POVERTY
OPPOSING VIEWPOINTS®

Other Books of Related Interest

OPPOSING VIEWPOINTS SERIES

Addiction
Chemical Dependency
Discrimination
Education
The Family
Health Care
The Homeless
Population
The War on Drugs
Welfare
Work

CURRENT CONTROVERSIES SERIES

Alcoholism
Developing Nations
Drug Abuse
Hunger
Marriage and Divorce
Poverty and the Homeless
Teen Pregnancy and Parenting

AT ISSUE SERIES

Alcohol Abuse
Genetically Engineered Foods
Single-Parent Families
Welfare Reform

POVERTY

OPPOSING VIEWPOINTS ®

Karen Balkin, *Book Editor*

Daniel Leone, *President*
Bonnie Szumski, *Publisher*
Scott Barbour, *Managing Editor*
Helen Cothran, *Senior Editor*

OPPOSING
VIEWPOINTS®
SERIES

GREENHAVEN
PRESS®

THOMSON
———————✦———————
GALE

San Diego • Detroit • New York • San Francisco • Cleveland
New Haven, Conn. • Waterville, Maine • London • Munich

LIBRARY OF CONGRESS CATALOGING-IN-PUBLICATION DATA

Poverty : opposing viewpoints / Karen Balkin, book editor.
    p. cm. — (Opposing viewpoints series)
Includes bibliographical references and index.
ISBN 0-7377-1698-3 (pbk. : alk. paper) — ISBN 0-7377-1697-5 (lib. : alk. paper)
    1. Poverty—United States. 2. Poor—United States. 3. Hunger—United States.
4. Medically uninsured persons—United States. 5. Economic assistance,
Domestic—United States. 6. Public welfare—United States. 7. Poverty. 8. Poor.
9. Hunger. 10. Medically uninsured persons. I. Balkin, Karen, 1949– .
II. Opposing viewpoints series (Unnumbered)
HC110.P6.P63 2004
362.5'0973—dc21
                                                                    2003044861

Printed in the United States of America

"Congress shall make no law. . . abridging the freedom of speech, or of the press."

First Amendment to the U.S. Constitution

The basic foundation of our democracy is the First Amendment guarantee of freedom of expression. The Opposing Viewpoints Series is dedicated to the concept of this basic freedom and the idea that it is more important to practice it than to enshrine it.

Swallow your pride, It should be limited. People shouldn't be able to burn our flag legally.

Contents

Why Consider Opposing Viewpoints? 9

Introduction 12

Chapter 1: Is Poverty a Serious Problem?

Chapter Preface 17

1. Hunger Is a Serious Problem for America's Poor 19
   Food First

2. Hunger Is Not a Serious Problem for America's
   Poor 24
   Robert Rector

3. The Uninsured Poor Suffer Ill Health 28
   Dennis P. Andrulis

4. Lack of Health Insurance Does Not Cause Ill
   Health Among Poor People 37
   Tom Miller

5. Homelessness Is a Serious Problem for Poor
   People 47
   America

6. Homelessness Is Not a Serious Problem for
   Poor People 51
   Leo K. O'Drudy III

Periodical Bibliography 55

**Chapter 2: What Are the Causes of Poverty in
America?**

Chapter Preface 57

1. Illegitimacy Is a Primary Cause of Poverty 58
   Isabel V. Sawhill

2. Unmarried Mothers Are Unfairly Blamed for
   Poverty 65
   Susan Douglas and Meredith Michaels

3. Substance Abuse Causes Poverty 73
   Robert Kaestner

4. The Link Between Substance Abuse and Poverty
   Has Been Exaggerated   78
   Joint Center for Poverty Research

5. A Lack of Individual Responsibility Causes
   Poverty   82
   Joel Schwartz

6. A Lack of Opportunities Causes Poverty   88
   Ellen Mutari

7. Housing Discrimination Causes Poverty   94
   Gregory D. Squires

8. Housing Discrimination Has Been Exaggerated   104
   John Hood

Periodical Bibliography   111

**Chapter 3: How Can Poor People in the United
States Be Helped?**

Chapter Preface   114

1. Government Programs Help the Poor   116
   Wendell Primus and Kathryn Porter

2. Government Programs Have Not Helped the
   Poor   122
   J.D. Tuccille

3. Increasing the Minimum Wage Can Help the
   Working Poor   126
   Holly Sklar

4. Increasing the Minimum Wage Is
   Counterproductive   130
   Thomas Sowell

5. Welfare Reform Is Effective   134
   U.S. Department of Health and Human Services

6. Welfare Reform Harms the Poor   138
   Debra Watson

7. Promoting Marriage Will Help End Poverty   142
   Wade F. Horn

8. Promoting Marriage Will Not Help End Poverty   148
   Jeanne Winner

Periodical Bibliography   153

Chapter 4: Is Worldwide Poverty a Serious Problem?

Chapter Preface 156

1. Global Poverty Causes Terrorism 158
   Strobe Talbott

2. Global Poverty Does Not Cause Terrorism 162
   Jane R. Eisner

3. Globalization Is Helping to Reduce World
   Poverty 167
   Ian Vásquez

4. Globalization Is Making World Poverty Worse 175
   Antonia Jubasz

5. High Population Growth Is Exacerbating World
   Poverty 180
   Population Reports

6. The World Can Sustain Its Growing Population 185
   Nicholas Eberstadt

7. Genetically Modified Crops Are Helping to
   Reduce World Hunger 189
   Willy De Greef

8. Genetically Modified Crops Are Not Reducing
   World Hunger 195
   John Robbins

Periodical Bibliography 200

For Further Discussion 201
Organizations to Contact 205
Bibliography of Books 212
Index 215

Why Consider Opposing Viewpoints?

"The only way in which a human being can make some approach to knowing the whole of a subject is by hearing what can be said about it by persons of every variety of opinion and studying all modes in which it can be looked at by every character of mind. No wise man ever acquired his wisdom in any mode but this."

John Stuart Mill

In our media-intensive culture it is not difficult to find differing opinions. Thousands of newspapers and magazines and dozens of radio and television talk shows resound with differing points of view. The difficulty lies in deciding which opinion to agree with and which "experts" seem the most credible. The more inundated we become with differing opinions and claims, the more essential it is to hone critical reading and thinking skills to evaluate these ideas. Opposing Viewpoints books address this problem directly by presenting stimulating debates that can be used to enhance and teach these skills. The varied opinions contained in each book examine many different aspects of a single issue. While examining these conveniently edited opposing views, readers can develop critical thinking skills such as the ability to compare and contrast authors' credibility, facts, argumentation styles, use of persuasive techniques, and other stylistic tools. In short, the Opposing Viewpoints Series is an ideal way to attain the higher-level thinking and reading skills so essential in a culture of diverse and contradictory opinions.

In addition to providing a tool for critical thinking, Opposing Viewpoints books challenge readers to question their own strongly held opinions and assumptions. Most people form their opinions on the basis of upbringing, peer pressure, and personal, cultural, or professional bias. By reading carefully balanced opposing views, readers must directly confront new ideas as well as the opinions of those with whom they disagree. This is not to simplistically argue that everyone who reads opposing views will—or should—change his or her opinion. Instead, the series enhances readers' understanding of their own views by encouraging confrontation with opposing ideas. Careful examination of others' views can lead to the readers' understanding of the logical inconsistencies in their own opinions, perspective on why they hold an opinion, and the consideration of the possibility that their opinion requires further evaluation.

Evaluating Other Opinions

To ensure that this type of examination occurs, Opposing Viewpoints books present all types of opinions. Prominent spokespeople on different sides of each issue as well as well-known professionals from many disciplines challenge the reader. An additional goal of the series is to provide a forum for other, less known, or even unpopular viewpoints. The opinion of an ordinary person who has had to make the decision to cut off life support from a terminally ill relative, for example, may be just as valuable and provide just as much insight as a medical ethicist's professional opinion. The editors have two additional purposes in including these less known views. One, the editors encourage readers to respect others' opinions—even when not enhanced by professional credibility. It is only by reading or listening to and objectively evaluating others' ideas that one can determine whether they are worthy of consideration. Two, the inclusion of such viewpoints encourages the important critical thinking skill of objectively evaluating an author's credentials and bias. This evaluation will illuminate an author's reasons for taking a particular stance on an issue and will aid in readers' evaluation of the author's ideas.

It is our hope that these books will give readers a deeper understanding of the issues debated and an appreciation of the complexity of even seemingly simple issues when good and honest people disagree. This awareness is particularly important in a democratic society such as ours in which people enter into public debate to determine the common good. Those with whom one disagrees should not be regarded as enemies but rather as people whose views deserve careful examination and may shed light on one's own.

Thomas Jefferson once said that "difference of opinion leads to inquiry, and inquiry to truth." Jefferson, a broadly educated man, argued that "if a nation expects to be ignorant and free . . . it expects what never was and never will be." As individuals and as a nation, it is imperative that we consider the opinions of others and examine them with skill and discernment. The Opposing Viewpoints Series is intended to help readers achieve this goal.

David L. Bender and Bruno Leone,
Founders

Greenhaven Press anthologies primarily consist of previously published material taken from a variety of sources, including periodicals, books, scholarly journals, newspapers, government documents, and position papers from private and public organizations. These original sources are often edited for length and to ensure their accessibility for a young adult audience. The anthology editors also change the original titles of these works in order to clearly present the main thesis of each viewpoint and to explicitly indicate the opinion presented in the viewpoint. These alterations are made in consideration of both the reading and comprehension levels of a young adult audience. Every effort is made to ensure that Greenhaven Press accurately reflects the original intent of the authors included in this anthology.

Introduction

"Poverty wears different masks in different places. We think of poverty as a city disease. But almost half of American poverty is found in our rural areas."
—President Lyndon B. Johnson, Conference on
Women in the War on Poverty, May 8, 1967.

The word *poverty* may conjure up images of rundown city blocks with condemned buildings and ragged homeless people, and, in fact, this vision is a reality in cities throughout the world. But rural poverty should come to mind as well since it is an even greater scourge in the United States and across the globe. While international experts often refer to the "urbanization of poverty" that took place in the twentieth century—there was a large population shift toward cities in the past hundred years—three-quarters of the world's poor (about 0.9 billion people) still live in rural areas. In the United States rural poverty rates have been consistently higher than urban rates for more than fifty years. According to the 2000 Census, about 11.3 percent of all Americans and 10.8 percent of urban citizens live in poverty. However, 13.4 percent of rural Americans live below the poverty line. Globally, 244 of the 250 poorest countries are predominantly rural.

While statistics may help define the dimensions of non-urban poverty, only a basic understanding of the rural poor and the causes of their condition can provide a true picture of rural poverty's significance, both nationally and globally. Poor rural people in the United States have less formal schooling than their urban counterparts and receive less regular health care. Further, they are more likely to be white and living in households of two or more adults with at least one adult working. They may or may not be engaged in farming activities and rarely own their own land. About 11.5 percent of rural households experienced hunger in 2000, a cruel irony since the majority of rural poor live in farming regions that feed the nation. Typically, they live in small towns and earn a living from low-skill, low-wage jobs in service areas, manufacturing, and extraction industries such as fishing or logging. Low population densities in rural areas are largely responsible for the lack of available employment, social services, and critical infrastructure such as quality schools and public transportation. This is especially true in areas of persistent poverty concentrated in Appalachia, the Mississippi Delta, the Rio Grand Valley, and on Native American reservations.

Homelessness, a common consequence of poverty wherever it exists, takes on a different character in rural areas. Shelters, the mainstay of the urban homeless, are rare in rural settings. Like day care centers, clinics, and programs for the elderly, they are among the social services lacking in sparsely populated rural areas underfunded by state and federal programs. Instead, rural people who find themselves homeless are more likely to move in with friends or relatives in overcrowded or substandard housing, or live in a car or camper. Studies comparing urban and rural homeless populations have found that homeless people in rural areas are more likely to be white, female, married, currently working at a low-wage job, homeless for the first time, and homeless for a shorter period of time.

In contrast to the rural poor in America, poor people in rural areas in sub-Saharan Africa, South and East Asia, Latin America, and the Caribbean are usually subsistence farmers for whom hunger is a constant threat and clean water is a rarity. They grow at least a portion of the food they eat and may own a few animals such as chickens or goats; they usually do not own the land on which they work or live. Typically, they work marginal land that has been degraded by overuse. In coastal areas, poor farmers supplement their income by fishing, and poor fishermen supplement their income by farming. While the demographics vary from country to country, overall, rural children living in poverty outnumber adults; women living in poverty outnumber men. This is due in part to male migration to cities where men are more likely to find work than are women.

Rural poverty in all parts of the world, including the United States, is not gender-neutral. For example, poor women in rural areas of Africa, Asia, and India have less access to land, credit, technology, education, and skilled work.

Moreover, their earnings are based on more menial and less self-directed work. In general women receive less health care and suffer the increased physical and emotional burdens of frequent pregnancies and child deaths. This added stress makes it all the more difficult for women to pull themselves out of poverty. Even in those areas where they are not substantially poorer than men, women are more likely to remain poor. In great part this is a consequence of illiteracy. Seventy percent of poor rural women in India are illiterate. Illiteracy is also prevalent among poor women in South Asia and China. Interestingly, studies in Kenya showed that if poor women received some education through an agricultural extension program, they used land more productively than men. It has been estimated that giving women one year of education could lead to a 24 percent increase in crop yields.

Addressing rural poverty is difficult because the problem is deeply entrenched and often overshadowed by issues surrounding urban poverty. "The legacy of history and the long marginalization of poor groups in terms of the distribution of land and other assets, in terms of institutions and of centuries of inequity in access to education, nutrition and health, create too great an obstacle . . . a majority of the poor will continue to be in rural areas well into the twenty-first century," according to Fawzi H. Al-Sultan, president of the International Fund for Agricultural Development (IFAD), a specialized financial agency of the United Nations created to combat hunger and rural poverty in developing nations. In the past most countries, including the United States, viewed rural poverty simply as a precursor to urban poverty—poor people left rural regions seeking more opportunities in cities that often could not provide them. Thus, solutions for dealing with poverty developed as solutions for dealing with urban poverty. However, as statistics on the extent of rural poverty show, efforts to address poverty must focus on helping the world's rural poor as well.

The United States and other countries are now working together to find solutions to the complex problem of rural poverty. *Poverty: Opposing Viewpoints* considers this and other related issues in the following chapters: Is Poverty a Serious

Problem? What Are the Causes of Poverty in America? How Can Poor People in the United States Be Helped? Is Worldwide Poverty a Serious Problem? Authors in these chapters debate the causes and effects of poverty in the United States and across the globe as they search for solutions that will help the world's poor.

CHAPTER 1

Is Poverty a Serious Problem?

Chapter Preface

"People in Africa are hungry," American mothers tell their well-fed children, then add, "clean your plates." Unfortunately, hunger is much closer than Africa. In 2000 a U.S. Department of Agriculture (USDA) report showed that 5.6 million adults and 2.7 million children, 3.3 million households, were classified as "hungry." Chronic hunger occurs when money is scarce, but starvation is rare in the United States because established programs, such as food stamps, help provide a safety net for poor families. "Food Stamps are *the* safety net program," says Beatrice Rogers, dean of academic affairs at the Gerald J. and Dorothy R. Friedman School of Nutrition, Science and Policy at Tufts University and acting director of Tufts's Center on Hunger, Poverty and Nutrition Policy. "The reason is that Food Stamps constitute the only program in the food safety net for which people are eligible simply because they are poor. Food Stamps give you purchasing power for food based not on your sex, not on your age, not on your family status, but simply on being poor. It's the first line of defense. Anyone is eligible for Food Stamps who needs them," she says.

The Food Stamp Program began as a group of pilot projects initiated by then-President John F. Kennedy in 1961. Although the food stamp Act of 1964 authorized the program as a permanent national policy, participation was voluntary on a county by county basis. Gradually, the USDA developed the administrative structure and working relationship with the states that made it possible to expand the program. At first, food stamps were purchased for a fraction of their full value by low-income families who redeemed them at local markets. Grocers were reimbursed by the federal government for the full value of the food stamps. "Food Stamps were perceived as a blend of free enterprise and welfare," said Jim Springfield, director of the Food Stamp Program in 1969. "To grocers, we emphasized that providing assistance through 'normal channels of trade' gave their customers more buying power."

The Food Stamp Program grew rapidly as nonparticipating counties signed up, realizing that food stamps allowed lower-income residents to buy more with the savings they reaped from using food stamps. In December 1969 there were 3.6 million people receiving food stamps; by November 1970 that number had grown to 9.3 million. Beginning in 1977, participants were no longer required to pay for a portion of their food stamps; this opened the program to some of the nation's neediest people. Food stamp participation continued to rise—hitting 19 million in 1989 and peaking at 24 million in 1994.

However, food stamp enrollment declined sharply to 17.2 million in 2000. Unfortunately, this decline did not mean there were fewer hungry people in the United States. On the contrary, emergency food aid requests from food banks increased. Eric M. Bost, USDA undersecretary for Food, Nutrition and Consumer Services, suggests that the decline in food stamp usage was due to the complexity of rules and forms that required an average of two trips and five hours for the initial filing and two hours for each rectification. Perhaps minimum-wage working families who comprise an increasing number of food stamp recipients simply could not take time from their jobs to complete the necessary paperwork and turned to privately funded food banks instead for help. USDA figures show that only 30 percent of the people seeking aid from food banks are also food stamp recipients. Welfare reform in 1996 also created some confusion regarding eligibility—some recipients who were cut from the welfare rolls thought they were also ineligible for food stamps. Further, some recipients became ineligible due to increases in income and assets that place them above the eligibility requirements. While the number of participants varies from year to year, food stamps continue to be the first line of defense against hunger for millions of low-income Americans.

Hunger in the richest nation in the world is just part of the paradox of American poverty. Together with homelessness and ill health, it creates a dehumanizing triad that millions struggle with daily. Authors in the following chapter explore these three issues as they wrestle with the problems of poverty in the United States.

"In the world's richest nation, more than 36 million people, including 14 million children, experience hunger."

Hunger Is a Serious Problem for America's Poor

Food First

In the following viewpoint, Food First contends that poverty, not food scarcity, is the reason that more than 36 million Americans are hungry. The United States produces more than enough food for everyone, it maintains. However, many poor families, even those with a working adult, often do not earn enough to buy adequate food. The institute argues that freedom from hunger is a basic human right that the U.S. government must guarantee to all its citizens. Food First is a nonprofit think tank and education-for-action center committed to ending hunger and poverty.

As you read, consider the following questions:
1. According to the institute, what does it mean to be "food insecure"?
2. What does the institute maintain is the leading cause of hunger?
3. Who decides who gets to eat in the United States, according to Food First?

The United States has never grown so much food. Scarcity is down, food is cheap, and enough food is produced to provide for every woman, man, and child. *Yet, in the world's richest nation, more than 36 million people, including 14 million children, experience hunger.*

The United States Department of Agriculture (U.S.D.A.) reports that in 2000, twelve percent of all American households were "food insecure." In other words, 1 in 10 households could not lead active, healthy lives because they did not have enough to eat. Of these families, 4.2 million households (8.5 million people) had to skip or reduce their meals.

Many Americans Are Hungry

Not surprisingly, those most likely to face hunger are the most vulnerable in our society: families with poverty-level incomes, single mothers and children, and the elderly.

The U.S.D.A. reports that in 2000, nearly 1 in 5 children (10 million) went hungry. Almost 3 million kids endured a more severe form of hunger—they ate less or skipped meals.

Proportionally, African-American and Latino households suffered from hunger more often than the national average. Some 7.7 million African-American families and over 8 million Latino families worried about food.

The greatest number of Americans going hungry were Caucasians. In 2000, over 16 million Caucasian Americans did not have enough to eat, and 4.5 million skipped meals or reduced portions.

America's Disappeared

The unprecedented economic growth of the 1990s should have lifted all boats, but studies reveal that the boom economy only lifted yachts.

In 2000, over 11 percent of the U.S. population, 34 million people lived in poverty. The average person fell deeper below the poverty line that year than ever before on record. Sixteen percent of all children live in poverty in the U.S. In 2000, the federal government's official poverty level for a family of four was $17,463—an egregiously inadequate amount [for] a family. . . . There's no rocket science to why the number of people living in poverty parallels the number of people going hungry. Without enough money to eat, people will go hungry. . . .

And how has the U.S. government responded to growing poverty and hunger in America? With a welfare reform law that erased a vital safety net for people experiencing financial hardship. Studies have shown that even full-time working families who left welfare do not earn enough in wages to move out of poverty. . . .

Mayors' Annual Survey on Hunger and Homelessness in American Cities

- Officials in the survey cities estimate that during the year 2000 requests for emergency food assistance increased by an average of 17 percent, with 83 percent of the cities registering an increase. This 17% increase in demand for emergency food is the second highest rate of increase since 1992. (The 1999 rate of 18% equaled the 1992 rate.)

- Requests for food assistance by families with children increased by an average of 16 percent—the highest rate of increase since 1991. Requests for emergency food assistance by elderly persons increased by an average of nine percent during the last year, with 75 percent of the cities reporting an increase.

- Sixty-two percent of the people requesting emergency food assistance were members of families—children and their parents. Thirty-two percent of the adults requesting food assistance were employed.

- In 100 percent of the cities, families and individuals relied upon emergency food assistance both in emergencies and as a steady source of food over long periods of time.

U.S. Conference of Mayors, *Status Report on Hunger and Homelessness*, December 14, 2000.

Second Harvest, the nation's largest network of emergency food providers, reports that in 2001, 23.3 million poor and working people across the country sought emergency food. But even working families did not earn enough to buy food: 40 percent had at least one working adult in their household.

More Requests for Emergency Food

Of the 23.3 million seeking emergency food, more than a third were children under the age of 18. Of these children, 9 percent were 5 years old and younger. [Eleven percent of those seeking emergency food] were the elderly. Similar to national hunger statistics, the majority of people needing food were Caucasian, 35 percent African-American, and 17 percent Latino.

In a survey of cities, the U.S. Conference of Mayors found that requests for emergency food assistance increased by 17 percent in 2001, but 13 percent of those seeking food had to be turned away. Food banks reported that they had to either reduce bags of food or turn people away.

Leading causes of hunger [were] low-paying jobs, followed by unemployment, the high cost of housing, and changes in the food stamp program, according to the U.S. Conference study. Forty-five percent of clients had to choose between paying for food or utilities, 35 percent had to choose between paying for food or rent, and 30 percent had to choose between paying for food or medical care.

Lack of Food Causes Health Problems

Hunger and malnutrition affect individual health, particularly that of young children. In 1996, there were 7.3 deaths per 1,000 live births, with black infants dying at double the rate of white infants. Infant mortality is closely linked with malnutrition due to a lack of nutritious food.

Hungry children suffer from two to four times as many individual health problems (such as fatigue, headaches, irritability, inability to concentrate, and frequent colds). Children who go to school on an empty stomach do not have the ability to learn in school because they cannot concentrate or excel on tasks they need to perform to learn the basics. This in turn leads to lost knowledge, brainpower, and productivity for our nation today and in the future. Hunger afflicts not only poor children and their families—it threatens the future of the U.S.

Freedom from Hunger Is a Right

When we think of "human rights" in the U.S., we often think of protecting individual rights. But we may be the only country in the world that blames the individual for being too poor to eat. It is time to address the core problems of hunger and poverty, instead of denying the existence of political solutions to economic injustice. Over the past thirty years, we have, as a nation, tolerated wider income disparities and deeper levels of hunger and poverty than any other developed nation. For our children's sake, this must stop. . . .

Right now, the millionaires in the Senate decide who gets to eat in the U.S. We can be a nation that allows our children to skip meals, or we can be a nation that prides itself on ensuring that everyone, regardless of their lot in life, has the right to be free from hunger.

Hunger is a measuring stick to judge the extent to which societies meet the needs of their people. With 36 million suffering from hunger, the U.S. is failing on its commitments to upholding the universal human rights of Americans.

Let's be consistent in our support of human rights by supporting the most basic human right of all here at home. In the wealthiest nation in the world, it's a shame 36 million Americans go hungry.

"Far from being a crisis, hunger is a limited problem, and one that usually doesn't last very long."

Hunger Is Not a Serious Problem for America's Poor

Robert Rector

In the following viewpoint, Robert Rector argues that hunger in America is a minor, temporary problem that has been highly exaggerated by activist groups. Most Americans, Rector maintains, are well nourished. He contends that the diets of poor children are nearly identical in protein, vitamin, and mineral content to those of middle-class children. Further, the diet-related health problems poor people face are due to overeating rather than a lack of food, he maintains. Robert Rector is a senior research fellow at the Heritage Foundation, a conservative public policy research institute.

As you read, consider the following questions:

1. According to Rector, what percentage of American families say that they have enough to eat?
2. In the author's opinion, what ironic fact does the government data about hunger reveal?
3. When temporary hunger does occur, what is usually the cause, according to the author?

Robert Rector, "Today's Special: Another 'Hunger Crisis,'" www.heritage.org, November 21, 2000. Copyright © 2000 by The Heritage Foundation. Reproduced by permission.

It's Thanksgiving, and political activists are serving up a familiar dish: cries of alarm about a "hunger crisis" in America. The Chicago-based group America's Second Harvest, for example, says millions of American children suffer from hunger. The Food Research and Action Center claims that 29 percent of all U.S. children—nearly one out of every three—is hungry or "at risk" of hunger.

But such startling claims are refuted by the federal government's own data. Surveys conducted by the Department of Health and Human Services show that 96 percent of American families report that they have "enough food to eat." About 3 percent say they "sometimes" don't have enough food. Only one half of 1 percent say they "often" don't have enough food.

These data also reveal an ironic fact: Nearly half of the people who claim they lack food are overweight. In fact, obesity is most common among the tiny group claiming they "often" lack food.

Are one-third of U.S. children hungry? In reality, American children, both rich and poor, are remarkably well nourished. The average amount of protein, vitamins and minerals consumed by poor children is virtually identical with what middle-class children consume. In most cases, it greatly exceeds recommended norms. For example, poor children, on average, take in more than 200 percent of the "recommended daily allowance" of protein, a relatively expensive nutrient.

Poor Children Are Often Overweight

Health problems relating to the under-consumption of food are scarce among both poor and middle-class children. Thinness (low weight for height) and stunting (low height for age) are virtually non-existent among both groups. In fact, poor American children are simply giants by international or historic standards. By the time poor boys reach age 18, they are, on average, one inch taller and 10 pounds heavier than a middle-class boy of the same age in the late 1950s.

Poor Americans do face health problems related to diet, but these mainly stem from an *over*-consumption of food, not food scarcity. In a nation plagued by excess calories, the poor are most likely to be overweight. Nearly half of poor adult women are overweight compared to a third of non-poor women.

Medical experts have expressed concern over the growth of obesity among American children. Unfortunately, obesity is most common among poor children. A recent medical study of low-income black and Hispanic students in Central Harlem found that 25 percent were "obese," and more than half of that group was "super-obese."

America's Poor Eat Well

According to the US Department of Agriculture, America's "poor" do not differ substantially in the amount of food they consume compared to the upper half of the income earners. America's poor eat one-third more meat than the average German, twice as much as the British, and three times more than the Japanese. No wonder the former US Surgeon General, C. Everett Koop, is warning of an "obesity crisis."

Thomas J. DiLorenzo, *The Free Market*, January 2000.

Recently, the government's principal food program for children (Women, Infants and Children) issued a study claiming that it wasn't responsible for the alarming growth of obesity among poor children. Whenever you have the government's major feeding program denying responsibility for obesity among the poor, it seems reasonable to conclude that activist claims of a widespread "hunger crisis" are just a bit overblown.

Finally, many believe that lack of money forces poor people to eat low-quality diets deficient in nutrients and high in fat. But government survey data show that nutrient richness (the amount of vitamins, minerals and protein per calorie of food) is the same for poor and middle-class Americans. And the diets of poor people, on average, are no higher in fat than the diets of the middle class.

Hunger Is a Limited Problem

Some poor people, particularly in the inner city, do have diets that are very high in fat. But this problem can be blamed on the heavy consumption of take-out "fast food." A diet laden with "Big Macs" and "Super-Size Fries" isn't healthy, but it's hardly evidence of a food shortage or a lack of money to buy food.

I'm not suggesting that periodic hunger doesn't occur in America. But far from being a crisis, hunger is a limited problem, and one that usually doesn't last very long. For example, U.S. Department of Agriculture surveys show that, in the last month [October 2000], about one American child in 200 missed one or more meals due to the family's lack of money for food. This is a cause for concern, of course, but it is far short of a national epidemic.

More importantly, when temporary hunger does occur, it is often linked to behavioral problems that are far more troubling than simple food shortages. In the inner city, for example, up to 80 percent of children are born outside of marriage. Drugs and crime are rampant. Activist groups may think they're doing poor Americans a favor, but bogus claims of a "hunger crisis" only distract attention from these all-too-real problems.

*"Persons without insurance had a greater
likelihood of dying in the hospital."*

The Uninsured Poor Suffer Ill Health

Dennis P. Andrulis

In the following viewpoint, Dennis P. Andrulis argues that access to health care is critical to good health and almost impossible to obtain without public (Medicaid or Medicare) or private health insurance. He contends that the uninsured poor, many of whom are working and earn too much to qualify for Medicaid but not enough to purchase health insurance, experience more preventable hospitalizations because they lack access to regular medical care. Further, they are more likely to receive substandard care for medical injuries. Dennis P. Andrulis is a research professor at the State University of New York Health Sciences Center in Brooklyn.

As you read, consider the following questions:
1. According to Andrulis, which group is most likely to report limited access to health care?
2. What does Andrulis contend is essential to eliminating disparities in health status between rich and poor?
3. How does increasing access to health care help a pregnant minority woman have a healthier baby, in the author's opinion?

Dennis P. Andrulis, "Access to Care Is the Centerpiece in the Elimination of Socioeconomic Disparities in Health," *Annals of Internal Medicine*, vol. 129, September 1, 1998, pp. 412–16. Copyright © 1998 by *Annals of Internal Medicine*. Reproduced by permission.

The Institute of Medicine defines access to health care as "the timely use of personal health services to achieve the best possible outcomes." Achieving the objectives implied in this definition for socioeconomically disadvantaged populations has come to represent a serious, continual, and somewhat time-worn objective in the United States. Without a national health insurance program, society has tacitly accepted a piecemeal, incremental approach to improving the health care circumstances of these populations. Such an approach has shifted the focus of efforts to states, in which substantial variation in the percentage of persons without insurance for at least 12 months (the definition of "long term") belies a concurrent variation in insurance policies; in 1995, this rate ranged from 2.9% in Hawaii to 17.1% in Louisiana. At the same time, many continue to believe that if the financial barriers to health care could be lowered or eliminated, we could greatly reduce differences in the quality of health care as well as health care outcomes across socioeconomic groups. But would leveling the differences created by financial inequity really eliminate major disparities, or is this a shibboleth that masks more complex, deep-seated concerns that would continue to perpetuate great inequality in health care access and health status?

This paper supports the contention that action that successfully decreases financial barriers across socioeconomic groups will go a long way toward the substantial reduction of socioeconomic disparities in health. In so doing, it draws on selected reports from the vast literature that lead to these conclusions and puts in context the great health care benefit that could be derived from a leveling of financial differences.

Poverty, Lack of Insurance, and Health Adversity

The literature is replete with studies linking problems with health care access, differences across socioeconomic groups, and health consequences. As we approach the 21st century, reports indicate that the consequences of such disparities are increasing. For example, a summary report on children who live in poverty, a population with large numbers of uninsured, profiled the familiar litany of adverse consequences, including greater likelihood of receiving lower-quality care and dying in infancy. Moreover, as many as one in four children—the same proportion of children growing up in poverty in the United States—may face these and other adverse circumstances. Between 1979 and 1994, the number of children younger than 6 years living in poverty increased from 3.5 million to 6.1 million.

A 1997 report from the Center for Studying Health Systems Change also shows that disparities remain large and that their adverse impact may be growing. This survey-based study of almost 44,000 persons conducted in 1996 and 1997 found a familiar pattern: Families classified as low income were more likely than any other group to report decreased access to health care within the past 3 years. More than twice as many uninsured persons (43%) reported reduced access compared with persons who had private insurance (21%). In contrast, elderly persons, who are eligible for Medicare coverage, were the least likely to report reduced access.

Investigations of avoidable hospitalizations and emergency department use among uninsured persons and across socioeconomic groups show how this situation plays out in our health care system. An examination of California hospital discharge data found that, among other factors, poverty was correlated with higher rates of preventable hospitalization. The report also concluded that uninsured persons are likely to have greater difficulty than privately insured patients in accessing inpatient care. A 1997 report using National Hospital Discharge Survey data found that the number of potentially avoidable hospitalizations was far greater in middle-income and low-income populations than in the wealthiest populations; children were also affected by socioeconomic disparities in access. These findings led the authors to comment on the "striking class and racial differences in rates of potentially avoidable hospitalization." Using National Medical Care Utilization and Expenditure Survey data, Spillman found that the rate of nonemergency care for uninsured children was only 70% of the rate for those who were insured and that much less money was being spent on the uninsured population for inpatient and ambulatory care. According to the National Center for Health Statistics, nonurgent cases accounted for more than 50% of the 90,000,000 visits to U.S.

hospital emergency departments in 1992. Emergency departments are a well-established source of access to persons of lower socioeconomic status, who most often have no other recourse for care.

This aspect of our health care system sets us apart from other countries as well, with the related consequences falling squarely on those who have difficulty meeting their health care costs. A survey-based comparison of perceived access to health care among residents in the United States, Canada, and Germany conducted in 1994 and 1995 found that persons in the United States were most likely to report difficulties in obtaining and paying for their health services. In particular, the U.S. group reported greater likelihood of financially based access problems. In all, 20% of the U.S. group reported "serious" problems in paying medical bills in the past year. In addition, an estimated one third of the uninsured U.S. group reported financially based access problems, and almost two thirds reported delaying care because of such problems. Significant differences were found for access to specialists, diagnostic tests, and overall medical care.

Breaking the Link Between Poverty and Lack of Access

Obviously, many factors influence the health of individual persons, regardless of whether they are poor. Nonetheless, the ability to substantially improve access for low-income populations through elimination of financial barriers is probably a sine qua non when it comes to eliminating disparities in health status. The health care literature provides important evidence of the financial leveling effect—or the lack thereof—by two measures: health care utilization and health care outcomes. For example, in an international study of children and health care utilization, C. Casanova and B. Starfield found that when access to primary care is leveled across income strata, no significant differences by income appeared for rates of ambulatory care-sensitive conditions, such as asthma. The implication drawn from this finding is that the ability to use a primary care practitioner may obviate worsening of a treatable condition that if left unaddressed, would probably require more urgent care. A survey-based examination of the link between access and insurance in the Seattle–King County area found that being insured was the strongest predictor for having a regular source of care and was strongly correlated with ease of access to care. Moreover, when uninsured persons became eligible for Medicaid, their health care access improved (although it never reached the levels seen with private insurance).

Health Depends on Wealth

The fact is: poverty kills. It is a reliable general rule that the poorer you are, the shorter your life span; the richer you are, the longer you live. For instance, a very poor person (in the lowest 10% of income) will die about 10 years sooner than people whose income puts him in the highest 10%. In fact, among the poor, poverty is responsible for more premature deaths than smoking or heart disease or cancer.

Larry Laudan, *Consumers' Research*, November 1996.

An examination of patterns of inpatient, outpatient, and related health care status among 346 persons who were previously uninsured and became enrolled in a Kaiser managed care program found patterns of utilization similar to those seen in a commercially enrolled group. In addition, the costs of care for this previously uninsured group were not substantially greater than those in the commercially enrolled group. A review of 1987 data from the National Medical Expenditures Survey and the Survey of Income and Program Participation from 1984 to 1988 found that persons receiving Aid to Families with Dependent Children who received Medicaid coverage were significantly more likely to use both inpatient and outpatient services than they would if they had been uninsured. Other evidence of the value of access comes from research examining health-related quality-of-life outcomes for HIV-infected low-income and medically indigent persons. Using interviews on access from 196 public hospital clinic patients participating in the HIV Outcomes Study, the authors found significantly better quality-of-life outcomes (such as freedom from pain and improved social and cognitive function) among persons who were in moderate physical and mental health and had greater access to services than those of similar health but with poorer access (access measures were based on Medical Outcomes Study responses).

Several studies have documented the adverse effect of lack of health insurance on outcomes and quality of care. A 1991 report by J. Hadley and colleagues comparing privately insured and uninsured hospital patients according to admission, use of resources, and discharge outcome found that with few exceptions, persons without insurance had a greater likelihood of dying in the hospital. A 1993 study by P. Franks and associates found lack of health insurance to be more highly correlated with death among adults who were followed over several years.

A report on birth outcomes in ethnic minority women suggests the positive outcome that can be derived from reducing financial access barriers. For eligible Medicaid recipients, a New Jersey initiative increased the number of prenatal visits available; increased provider reimbursement; and enhanced other service support, including follow-up after pregnancy, case coordination, and health education. Program evaluation found an increase of almost 56 g[rams] in mean birth weight and a 3.7% reduction in the likelihood of having a low-birth-weight infant. Because low birth weight is associated with more problems in children, the ability to increase perinatal weight through improved access to health care implies healthier outcomes for a population of concern.

Uninsured Patients Receive Substandard Care

A 1997 cross-national health care comparison quantified how limited health financing adversely affects the ability to improve access and outcomes for U.S. residents. As of 1960, only 4 of the 29 Organization of Economic Development and Cooperation nations—the United States, Turkey, Portugal, and Greece—had fewer than 50% of their citizens eligible for inpatient hospital care within a public system. By 1995, only the United States remained below the 50% level. These statistics are linked with the finding that the U.S. ranking in infant mortality worsened to 12th from 23rd of 27 countries in 1960. A change in rank for the worse was also seen with life expectancy, which moved from 20th to 13th in this time period.

Other reports have documented the adverse effect of decreased financial access on health care quality, with implications for health outcomes. A New York study examining the relation between socioeconomic status and quality of care found that uninsured persons were more likely to receive substandard health services for medical injury. A Boston-based hospital study found that uninsured persons received fewer procedures and had shorter inpatient stays than privately or publicly insured patients. Such results may be an indicator of substandard health care.

A study of hypertension among more than 200 ethnic minority patients in New York found that greater severity of condition was significantly related to absence of a relationship with a primary care provider. Moreover, those without health insurance had a greater tendency to use emergency departments for hypertension testing. The authors concluded that primary care access that is improved through health insurance can increase effectiveness in controlling hypertension among ethnic minority patients. Because hypertension has been linked to adverse outcomes, control of this condition suggests better health for these persons.

Leveling Health Insurance Inequality

The historical failure of national proposals to equalize financial access does not mean that no major examples of promising initiatives can be found. Rather, targeted interventions, as well as strategies intended to have a broader effect, provide some success stories or actions worth watching.

Recent breakthroughs in HIV treatment and related coverage expansions through Medicaid and other venues present one of the most dramatic examples of how action to reduce financial disparities in access can have a leveling effect on health care quality and outcomes across socioeconomic strata. The introduction of multidrug treatment regimens and, in particular, protease inhibitors greatly increased the ability to restore a high level of functioning in HIV-infected persons. For many, it not only means a better quality of life but also may literally be life-saving. The Centers for Disease Control and Prevention confirmed this dramatic change in its 1997 update on AIDS in the United States. The agency reported registering the first decrease in AIDS-related op-portunistic infections, crediting prevention strategies and the application of antiretroviral therapies. The Centers for Disease Control and Prevention noted in particular that in one of their Adult/Adolescent Spectrum of Disease projects, the proportion of patients receiving combination antiretro-viral therapy, including protease inhibitors, increased from 24% in the second part of 1995 to 65% in 1996.

The response of government and the private sector to date has led to the broad application of this regimen and notable success, thus graphically demonstrating a direct link between leveling the financial differences across socioeconomic groups and positive impact. In fact, the conclusion reached by one report bluntly stated, "The expense of these agents (protease inhibitors) may be offset by forestalling disease pro-gression and death and returning people to productive life." However, the situation remains precarious as the need among poor and nonpoor persons with HIV infection remains great and growing, and a more permanent solution to the financ-ing of HIV care, which costs as much as $10,000 per patient per year, is still unclear.

The lessons from AIDS and the new therapies should not be lost for other conditions. For example, a California study of prenatal care found that uninsured women were at the greatest risk for late visit initiation for prenatal care and in-adequate numbers of visits compared with women with Medicaid coverage and privately insured women. The au-thors concluded that attention should be directed in large part toward overcoming financial access barriers. A report on breast cancer according to insurance coverage reached similar conclusions on the consequences of lack of insur-ance—in this case, leading to a higher frequency of adverse outcomes, including lower survival rates. In this case, the au-thors concluded that a lack of insurance may have created barriers to critical primary care that are much less likely to occur among the privately insured. Implicit in these studies is the role that insurance coverage could play in providing access to care and improving outcomes for an array of con-ditions. In fact, on the progress evidenced by AIDS coverage by Medicaid and the lack of such coverage (and, thus, remaining barriers) for so many other conditions, bioethicist Arthur Caplan noted, "This disease-by-disease strategy is not fair and equitable.". . .

Disparities in Health Care Access Must End

Current deliberations on insurance, access, and outcomes continue a long-standing tradition in the United States. Managed care and greatly intensified competitive pressures have raised the stakes in the debate, threatening to drive an even deeper wedge between the more than 40,000,000 uninsured persons and those with insurance. In particular, the increasing emphasis on market advantage and financially covered lives and increasing intolerance of cost shifting among payers—one of the historical methods of covering the costs of care for uninsured persons—is creating potentially insurmountable disincentives for many providers to treat persons without insurance. Moreover, inadequate capitation rates could expand the number of uninsured persons. The consequence may be a large segment of U.S. residents relegated to sustained or worsening inequality in access and outcomes.

Any truly successful, long-term solution to the health problems of the nation will require attention at many points, especially for low-income populations who have suffered from chronic underservice if not outright neglect. But as for a single change that can have the greatest impact, our state governments, the federal government, and the U.S. Congress could not choose a better place to leave their mark than elimination of disparities in health care access between rich and poor.

"Access to health care may be responsible for only a relatively small part of health, with more important determinants being genetics, environment, and human behaviors."

Lack of Health Insurance Does Not Cause Ill Health Among Poor People

Tom Miller

In the following viewpoint, originally presented as part of a Cato Institute Policy Forum, Tom Miller argues that uninsured people manage to obtain adequate health care when they need it. Moreover, he contends that poverty and the uninsured status that usually accompanies it are not causes of poor health. Ill health among the poor, he maintains, is due to factors other than limited access to care, such as lack of education and unhealthy lifestyle practices. Tom Miller is director of Health Policy Studies at the Cato Institute.

As you read, consider the following questions:
1. According to Miller, why should the presumption that more health care is always good be challenged?
2. In the author's opinion, why do health habits (like smoking) vary with socioeconomic status?
3. What is the relationship between health and education, according to Miller?

Tom Miller, "Will More Health Insurance Improve Health Outcomes?" www.cato.org, June 19, 2002. Copyright © 2002 by the Cato Institute. Reproduced by permission.

As a general overview and warning, I would suggest you be skeptical of any and all sweeping claims about single factor explanations for what improves or impairs health status and health outcomes. In particular, we should reexamine the too facile presumption that more health care is always good, and, because it improves access to more health care, more health insurance coverage is always also desirable, if not necessary.

We need to be concerned with the appropriate measure of the bottom line by focusing on the output, not the input. Health insurance only provides value to the extent that it improves health outcomes, it improves our health status, and it protects us from serious financial risk.

Now, the assumption that health insurance affects health outcomes is a longstanding one, but also a relatively soft one. Consider that it may also be held much less due to persuasive evidence than as an act of faith, or even as a cover for self-interested parties seeking primarily to get paid more predictably and more adequately for their health services invoices. Nevertheless, we are in the midst of the latest wave of megastudies that purport to cement the connection between expanded health insurance coverage—financed by public subsidies—and improved health. The latest entrant is the study *Care Without Coverage: Too Little, Too Late*, by a committee of the Institute of Medicine (IOM). . . .

The study is the second of a series of six planned IOM studies along these lines. It aims to disabuse us of the notion that Americans without health insurance manage to get the care that they really need. It finds instead that working-age individuals without health insurance are more likely to receive too little medical care and receive it too late, be sicker and die sooner, and receive poorer care even when they're in the hospital for acute situations.

Distorted Statistics

Of course, you always need a headline grabber in this field, and this study furnished the factoid that more than 18,000 adults die each year in the U.S. because they are uninsured and can't get proper health care. Now, the study appears to compare working-age people with no health coverage at all with those who have relatively complete health insurance coverage. There is no noticeable effort to compare the outcomes of the uninsured with people who may have incomplete or limited coverage, such as catastrophic coverage.

There is also an earlier Institute of Medicine study which asked whether it's possible to sort out and disentangle the effects of race, socioeconomic status, and insurance coverage on health. Jennifer Haas and Nancy Adler, in October 2001, in what's called *The Causes of Vulnerability*, note that most studies have examined utilization of health care rather than health status as the outcome measure, and measures of health care utilization and process of care are more strongly and consistently influenced by insurance status than are measures of health status alone.

Other factors besides health insurance remain on the table as determinants of poor health, and they include low literacy, lifestyle practices, and health benefits. Haas and Adler find that the implementation of universal coverage in other countries may narrow disparities in health utilization but not disparities in health. Ethnic and socioeconomic disparities in health persist.

Despite mixed evidence at best, though, the paper then hurtles on to a conclusion that, given the political obstacles to other types of broad societal interventions that might attempt to reduce ethnic and socioeconomic disparities in health, health insurance may be a necessary first step toward improving health status in the U.S. In other words, why not take what the political defense gives you?

Current Studies Are Not Definitive

Also out in May 2002 is a lengthy study by Jack Hadley, of the Urban Institute, for the Kaiser Family Foundation, called *Sicker and Poorer: The Consequences of Being Uninsured.* It notes that none of the many studies it reviews on the positive relationships between health insurance, use of medical care, health, income, and education is definitive, nor are their findings universal.

Hadley suggests, though, we should distinguish between studies that suggest little or no health benefit from additional medical care use by well-insured populations and those studies suggesting that the uninsured would benefit from health insurance coverage and greater medical care use. . . .

Hadley attempts to address the Medicaid conundrum, which involves many studies finding that people covered by Medicaid tend to have worse health outcomes than the privately insured. Indeed, he notes that in some locations care paid for by Medicaid may not be very different from or better quality than care provided at no cost to the uninsured in public clinics and hospitals or that the uninsured . . . pay for themselves. After a lot of heavy lifting on the overall Medicaid issue, the jury, I think, remains out on that one. So Hadley then focuses more on the potential benefits of insurance for the uninsured working families who are not currently eligible for Medicaid.

Now, within the limits of mostly observational studies in this field, Hadley provides an estimated range of the quantitative effects of extending health insurance coverage to all the uninsured, and suggests that their mortality rates would decline by at least 5 percent. . . .

But on the health economist's other hand, sometimes including the more invisible hand of the market, a number of other studies raise many questions about the "more health insurance, better health care" connection. Not all those studies point in exactly the same direction and reach an integrated, mutually consistent set of conclusions, so a dose of humility and skepticism is in order across the board. But let's start out with a broadly accepted proposition—wealthier is healthier—or, even more broadly, individuals with a higher socioeconomic status have better health—and then we'll start going around in circles.

Socioeconomic Status Is Related to Health

We'll start with Ellen Meara, of Harvard Medical School. Her paper is called *Why Is Health Related to Socioeconomic Status? The Case of Pregnancy and Low Birth Weight*. She examined pregnancy and health at birth to investigate how socioeconomic status may be related to health. She found that it is the health habits and behaviors [that matter most]. . . .

A limited set of maternal health habits during pregnancy, particularly smoking habits, can explain about half of the correlation between socioeconomic status and low birth weight among white mothers and about one-third of the correlation among black mothers. In contrast, controlling for differential access to medical care and differences in pre-pregnancy maternal health status has no impact on differentials in health outcomes by socioeconomic status.

Well, why do health habits like smoking vary by socioeconomic status factors like education and income? It is most intriguing that Meara finds that education, as measured by differences in knowledge per se, and differences in how pregnant women use common knowledge, account for only about one-third of the difference in health behavior—in this case smoking. The much stronger factor in driving differences in smoking by socioeconomic status appears to be what she terms network effects at the family level, the impact of information and stigma received from those living and working near an individual, in influencing the degree to which those individuals make different investments in both health and education, such as not smoking while pregnant. . . .

Too Much Is Expected from Prenatal Programs for the Poor

Meara asks whether Medicaid spending on the poor represents the most effective way to reduce disparities in health. A number of health insurance expansions have lowered adverse outcomes among the poor, such as infant mortality, but through very intensive and very costly medical care interventions at birth, rather than preventing the prevalence of low birth weight and related conditions. She concludes that we may expect too much from prenatal programs for the poor. Infant health disparities by socioeconomic status are largely determined by disparities in health habits, and those disparities exist early in life. Even programs that redistribute income without affecting such third variables as time preferences, self-control, and stress may not improve infant health.

Next up, won't national health insurance reduce differences in health outcomes so that, really, money doesn't matter as much? Well, the closest U.S. version of national health insurance and universal coverage is Medicare, for nearly all Americans age 65 and over. But recent work by John Wennberg, Elliott Fisher and Jonathan Skinner, in *Health Affairs*, shows that Medicare spending varies more than twofold among different regions, and those variations persist even after differences in health are corrected for.

Higher Medicare levels are largely independent of beneficiaries' need for services. They are due largely to the increased use of supply-sensitive services, such as physician visits, specialist consultations, and hospitalizations. Higher spending in various regions does not result in more effective care or better health outcomes, but money still matters to those collecting it for providing and billing for increased levels of health services.

What about another international example? Orazio Attanasio, of the University College in London, and Carl Emmerson, of the Institute for Fiscal Studies, studied the relationship between socioeconomic status and health outcomes, or, more particularly, between mortality, health status, and wealth. They used data from the British Retirement Survey, controlling for initial health status. Attanasio and Emmerson found that wealth rankings are important determinants of mortality and health outcomes even in a country such as the United Kingdom, with universal government-run health care. . . .

Doctors Count More than Dollars

However, Jonathan Meer and Harvey Rosen of Princeton, along with Douglas Miller of the University of California at Berkeley, would caution against concluding that dollars count more than doctors and that significant health gains can be made with relatively moderate spending for income transfers to the poor. In their paper, *Exploring the Health-Wealth Nexus*, they use a more sophisticated instrumental variables procedures, with inheritance as an instrument for change in wealth. And they find no short-term impact of wealth on health, at least for as long as a five-year period.

If we want to close the health outcomes gap between rich and poor, and simply transferring money directly to poor people won't do the job, why not just throw more subsidies at the health care industry itself, so that more and better health care can be produced and then made available to everyone at lower prices? Well, let's take a look at what Dana Goldman and Darius Lakdawalla of RAND said in that regard.

They started in their paper, *Understanding Health Disparities Against Education Groups*, with the widely accepted consensus view that better educated people are healthier, but then they dug a little deeper to find that health disparities actually increase as the price of health inputs fall. Indeed, government subsidies for health care research, technological progress and, ironically, even universal health insurance, may worsen health inequality over time.

More Insurance Does Not Always Equal Better Health

Suppose that everyone gets insurance. Would people's health improve? For many uninsured, the answer is no, because they're already healthy. Two fifths of the uninsured are between 18 and 35. For most of them, insurance would protect against unexpected medical calamity. Children are an additional quarter of the uninsured. Most are fairly healthy. The real question is what happens to people with serious ailments. We don't know. No one doubts that insurance would prompt today's uninsured to visit doctors and hospitals more often. But how much this extra care would translate into better health is unclear.

Robert J. Samuelson, *Newsweek*, November 8, 1999.

What is really at work here is that the reductions in the price of health care, or expansions in the overall demand for health inputs, disproportionately benefit the well-educated. Technological progress also lowers the quality-adjusted price of health care.

All these price-reducing measures boost the overall level of health investment, which is then reflected in greater disparities across education groups. Those disparities are widest among sicker groups because they consume more health inputs. The chronically ill do learn more by doing, and they gain the most experience in controlling more of their own health investments. But, most of all, more educated people are more productive at managing their own health, and they are the first to adopt and benefit from new patient-intensive technologies.

More Schooling Improves Health

Goldman and Lakdawalla note that health inputs under an individual's control are more important than medically intensive inputs, and the educated use more self-managed care than the uneducated. So, if we run more escalating rounds of the medical arms race, the less educated will lag further behind and receive smaller shares of—dare I call it—trickle-down health care. But greater levels of schooling do improve health.

An apple a day for the teacher may keep the emergency room doctor away, but do only the dumb die young? Well, Adriana Lleras-Muney of Princeton has a new paper out in June 2002, called, *The Relationship Between Education and Adult Mortality in the United States*. It suggests not only that more education reduces mortality rates but the effect is much stronger than previously assumed.

For her experiment, she examined States that strengthened their compulsory schooling in child labor laws between 1915 and 1939. Depending on the measure she uses, an additional year of education lowers the probability of dying in the next 10 years by approximately 1.3 to 3.6 percentage points. She concludes that the benefits of education are large enough that we need to consider education policy more seriously as a means to increase health, especially in light of the fact that other factors, such as expenditures on health, have not been proven to be very effective. . . .

Health Worsens as the Economy Improves

If you are looking for another counterintuitive conundrum, consider questioning whether economic growth is bad for your health. Christopher Ruhm of UNC-Greensboro, in a paper called *Economic Expansions Are Unhealthy: Evidence from Microdata*, discovers a countercyclical variation in physical health that is especially pronounced for individuals of working age, and for employed persons and for males.

Most aspects of health worsen when the economy temporarily improves. Any reductions in stress during good economic times are more than offset by increases in workplace accidents and highway fatalities, increased smoking, reduced exercise, and heightened obesity. The negative health effects of economic expansions accumulate over several years and occur despite increased use of medical care. . . .

Finally, what about the largely unchallenged assumption that greater levels of health insurance coverage must be subsidized for those people who are less likely to be fully insured in order to increase their utilization of health care services and improve their health outcomes. Harvey Rosen and Craig Perry of Princeton, in a paper called *Insurance and the Utilization of Medical Services Among the Self-Employed,* analyzed how the self-employed and wage earners differ with respect to insurance coverage and utilization of various health care services.

They found that even though the self-employed received significantly smaller tax incentives to purchase health insurance and they accordingly are less likely to be insured, the self-employed are able to finance access to care from sources other than insurance. Their relative lack of health insurance does not substantially reduce their utilization of health care services, it does not create economic hardship, or have a negative impact either on their health or the health of their children.

Perry and Rosen suggest that access to health care may be responsible for only a relatively small part of health, with more important determinants being genetics, environment, and human behaviors. . . .

Expanding Insurance May Not Improve the Health of the Poor

Finally, we turn to Helen Levy again, with colleague David Meltzer of the University of Chicago, who ask, *What Do We Really Know About Whether Health Insurance Affects Health?* in a December 2001 paper. They note that very few of the hundreds of past studies establish a causal relationship between health insurance and health. They are largely dismissive of observational studies that, in their view, do not account for the difficulty of observing truly random variation on health insurance status for causal relationships that run in both directions and for other unobserved factors. . . .

But they acknowledge that health insurance and health are both complex, multidimensional goods that are measured imperfectly, that they only have a limited set of experimental and quasi-experimental studies on which to draw, and that their study stops short of establishing a downstream connection between access to medical care and delivery of medical care on health.

So, after blowing away most of the past studies analyzing health insurance and health, Levy and Meltzer conclude that there may be a small positive effect of health insurance on health outcomes on those populations most likely to be the targets of public coverage expansions, but that there is also evidence that in some cases expansions in health insurance may not result in measurable improvements in health. . . .

Levy and Meltzer admit they cannot say which interventions related to health insurance would be most effective in improving health. And they point out that expanding insurance is not the only way to improve health. So it remains unsettled as to whether money aimed at improving health would be better spent on expanded health insurance or other interventions that directly target health or access to medical care, such as inner-city clinics, community-based screening programs, or advertising campaigns to encourage nutrition.

"Homelessness in a prosperous United States is a disgrace."

Homelessness Is a Serious Problem for Poor People

America

In the following viewpoint, the editors of *America* argue that homelessness, while perhaps less visible than in previous years, is no less a problem today. In thirty of the country's largest cities, requests for emergency shelter increased 15 percent in 1998. The editors maintain that many of those living in shelters are working and still cannot afford to pay rent. Further, many local governments have added to the difficulties of homeless people by enacting quality of life laws aimed at criminalizing homelessness. *America* is a national Catholic magazine.

As you read, consider the following questions:
1. According to the editors, what percentage of homeless people are working?
2. What cities are cited by the National Law Center as having the "meanest streets"?
3. What do the editors maintain are the principal causes of homelessness?

D espite unprecedented prosperity, thousands of Americans are hungry and have no place to sleep at night. The U.S. Conference of Mayors' annual "Status Report on Hunger and Homelessness in American Cities," released in mid-December [1998], reports that in the past year emergency shelter requests were up 15 percent for families (11 percent overall), and requests for food assistance rose 14 percent.

Many of these homeless people are parents and their children. Children, in fact, make up a quarter of the homeless population. A number of studies have shown that the instability of their lives can lead to poor health, developmental delays and greater risks for anxiety and depression. Especially disturbing is the fact that requests for shelter and food cannot always be met; nearly a third of the families seeking shelter are turned away for lack of resources. In San Antonio, Texas, for example, families who can find no space in shelters sleep under bridges, in parks or in cars. Much the same bleak scenario holds true for food requests; because of the increased demand, emergency food agencies have frequently had to cut back both on the amounts distributed and on the number of times a month requests can be honored.

Twenty percent of those in shelters are employed either full or part-time. One of the painful ironies of the situation is that in a number of cities—such as Denver, Boston and Philadelphia—the strong economy has led landlords to raise rents. As a result, parents employed in low-wage jobs are unable to pay for rent, food and other necessities and therefore end up in shelters, not infrequently separated from their children. As Philadelphia officials put it with considerable understatement, "the rising economic tide is not lifting all boats." The survey blames welfare reform to some degree for its negative effect on both hunger and homelessness. People who have lost their welfare benefits have not always found jobs with salaries sufficient to cover living costs; and often they do not realize that they may still be eligible for food stamps and so do not apply for them. The mayors' report, however, considers the main causes of the increase in shelter populations and emergency food requests to be jobs that pay too little and the lack of affordable housing. Other causes include substance abuse and mental health problems that go unaddressed because of a lack of needed services like case management, housing and treatment.

Quality of Life Laws Hurt the Homeless

As if the difficulties of homeless people were not bad enough, another recent report—released in early January [1999] by the National Law Center on Homelessness & Poverty in Washington, D.C.—describes local governments' continuing efforts to enact stringent anti-homeless legislation. The report, entitled "Out of Sight—Out of Mind?", documents the increasing criminalization of homeless men and women. The very title tells much of the story; many local governments try to remove homeless people from the public eye as bad for business. This has been particularly true of New York City, with its large concentrations of homeless persons. There the mayor's emphasis on so-called quality of life crimes has meant that homeless men and women have increasingly been pushed from affluent sections of Manhattan into the poorer surrounding boroughs. Sweeps, the report states, "continue on almost a nightly basis."

Not surprisingly, the National Law Center's survey cites New York as one of five U.S. cities having the "meanest streets." The other four are Atlanta, Chicago, San Francisco and Tucson. But

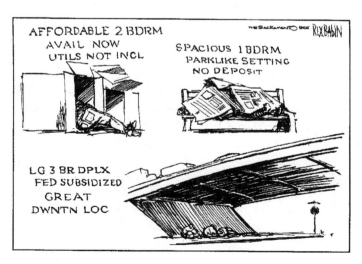

Babin. © 2002 by Rex Babin. Reprinted by permission.

the center's report also gives credit to several cities whose officials are taking more constructive approaches. Dallas, for instance, provides birth certificates to homeless people, even to those from out of state, as a way of assisting them to apply for public housing. Public housing applicants around the nation, though, face waiting lists that average two years in length. The waiting period for Section 8 certificates, which provide not only rental assistance but also wide freedom of choice as to where a family lives, is almost three years. Even when families are lucky enough to obtain Section 8 certificates, however, not all landlords will honor them—a sign of the stigma that dogs the lives of poor people throughout the nation.

Housing Vouchers Help

Estimates of the number of people who are homeless on any given night range between 600,000 and 760,000 nationwide. Funding to help the homeless has not kept pace with the growing need. Little wonder, then, that—despite an increase in shelter beds and food pantries—many requests for shelter and food go unmet. In addition, another advocacy group, the National Coalition for the Homeless, has pointed out that much of the existing funding focuses on emergency measures rather than on addressing the causes of homelessness. One hopeful sign is that, thanks to a substantial budget increase, the Department of Housing and Urban Development is now able to provide housing vouchers for 90,000 more families.

Although the causes of homelessness are complex, the principal ones remain jobs that do not pay a living wage, inadequate financial assistance for those who cannot work, insufficient medical care for the mentally ill and addicted, and the lack of affordable housing. Until these are addressed, homelessness will be neither out of sight nor out of mind. Indeed, in its prediction for the new year, the mayors' survey found that almost all the 30 cities surveyed expect the demand for emergency shelter and food to quicken. Hunger and homelessness in a prosperous United States is a disgrace. Voters need to tell their local, state and national leaders that careful planning and funding must be focused on caring for these people in need. Trying to make them invisible is no solution.

"By far most 'homeless' people are exactly what they seem: lazy, addicted or insane."

Homelessness Is Not a Serious Problem for Poor People

Leo K. O'Drudy III

In the following viewpoint, Leo K. O'Drudy III argues that the majority of homeless people are too lazy to work, addicted, or insane. He maintains that few honest, hardworking people ever become homeless—and if they do it is only for a short time. According to O'Drudy, identifying with the homeless will cause Americans to be fearful and doubt the virtues of capitalism. He contends that liberal politicians and judicial decisions are responsible for public policies sympathetic to undeserving homeless people; most of the homeless should be arrested or confined to mental hospitals. O'Drudy is a contributor to *Human Events*.

As you read, consider the following questions:

1. In the author's opinion, why is the word "homeless" misleading?
2. According to O'Drudy, who has changed the character of America's urban centers?
3. In addition to liberal politicians and jurists, who does the author maintain is responsible for the homeless situation?

I have worked here in Washington, D.C., for about six years now. For much of that time, every morning, there has been a shabby, crazy woman in tiger-striped makeup who camps herself out beside a magnificent statue of Christopher Columbus that stands between Union Station and the Capitol.

Smack in the path of a heavy stream of foot traffic, she is the first impression thousands of visitors from around America and all over the globe have of Washington. She has been there through most, if not all, of Bill Clinton's presidency, vanishing every winter only to reappear every spring.

Many conservative commentators have been predicting a sudden resurgence of interest in "homelessness" by the liberal media and their allies in political office. After the endless caterwauling we heard about this issue under Presidents Ronald Reagan and George Bush, which contrasts sharply with the utter silence about it while Bill Clinton was President, it will indeed be interesting to see whether that old political weapon of the left is hauled out and used once again against the new President George W. Bush.

If a Republican has been in office for a while, the existence of "homelessness" must become his fault, and his failure to solve the problem will be blamed on his supposed cruelty and hatred for the weak.

I think these predictions are probably right. And conservatives need to prepare for this onslaught.

The Word "Homeless" Deliberately Misleads

The first thing for us to remember and repeat is that the very terms "homeless" and "homelessness" are politically correct euphemisms, which is to say, lies. They are lies because they are deliberately misleading; they lead one's attention to a peripheral problem (the lack of a home) instead of the central problems (drinking and drug abuse, mental illness, and old-fashioned sloth).

The crazy mumbling men I see every evening, or the healthy men who have decided to lie around outside during the day or bother honest people making their way to and from work (read: bums), will not become model citizens if they are suddenly presented with the keys to a home.

If that sort of thing worked, public housing would be the safest and nicest areas to live in.

Why, then, are they called "homeless" instead of "bums," "winos," and "mentally unbalanced"? Because we are meant to be convinced that, but for a few paychecks, we could be those people. Thus, we should feel fear for the future, doubt about the justice of free enterprise capitalism, and, most importantly, shame for our civilization and way of life. This helps push along the politically correct agenda, and to preserve the welfare state.

Ending Homelessness

Should society finally decide to end street vagrancy, it could go far in that direction by facilitating commitment to mental hospitals and enforcing existing laws against street living. Though the average householder would surely welcome such a say in these matters; a vocal minority purporting to represent the interests of the homeless governs homeless policy.

Heather MacDonald, *The Wall Street Journal*, November 17, 1997.

Sometimes, yes, someone otherwise honest and hard-working falls into misfortune, loses his home or can't pay his rent, and sleeps in his car or at a church shelter for a while until he gets back on his feet. But the publicity accorded such cases is misleadingly disproportionate. By far most "homeless" people are exactly what they seem: lazy, addicted or insane.

My father grew up in New York City in the 1930s. The Great Depression, the most crushing economic collapse in many lifetimes, was a daily reality. As a child he roamed all over the city via its trolleys and subways. And yet, he never saw people sleeping on grates and benches, wandering around draped in blankets, camped out in front of every subway stop. Nor did the vast majority of urban Americans. Such things were unheard of.

The Left Is Responsible

Beggars just hanging around or pestering honest people in the streets was something every American associated with faraway lands, cities like Cairo, Mexico City, Calcutta. That's why Washington, D.C., today, and other American cities, are still a shock for my father. The character and fabric of daily life in America's urban centers, even our financial, shopping, government, and recreational districts, has changed dramatically for the worse.

Left-wing politicians and, to a great degree, left-wing judicial activism, are responsible for this collapse. Generations ago, police officers would simply arrest vagrants for violating laws against, well, vagrancy. And those not in their right minds were kept in mental hospitals and given treatment.

Once the left was finished, however, the mentally ill could not be detained or treated against their will if they were deemed not a danger to themselves or others. And great solicitous care was taken for the rights of bums; now a paper bag surrounding a bottle of rotgut cannot be opened by the police as proof that a wino is violating the city's ban on drinking in public, not without a search warrant.

And the parks and sidewalks of America's cities take on the character of miserable Third World slums. The left has much to answer for, especially its cohorts on the federal bench who legislate rather than interpret, as well as the media that continue to blame "homelessness" on "selfish" conservatives.

And that's the second thing we should remember to speak up about when the liberals begin the "homeless" game again.

Periodical Bibliography

The following articles have been selected to supplement the diverse views presented in this chapter.

Gill Donovan	"Mayors Find Hunger Increasing in Their Cities," *National Catholic Reporter*, December 28, 2001.
John W. Fountain	"On a Back Road, Stuck in Poverty," *New York Times*, November 21, 2002.
Mark Goldblatt	"Enforcing Civility," *National Review Online*, January 21, 2002. www.nationalreview.com.
Robert Greenberg	"The Painful Reality of Hunger," *Archives of Pediatrics and Adolescent Medicine*, May 1998.
David H. Holben	"An Overview of Food Security and Its Measurement," *Nutrition Today*, July/August 2002.
Sarah Kimble	"Charity Care Programs: Part of the Solution or Part of the Problem?" *Public Health Reports*, September 2000.
David Lawrence	"Class, Racial Bias in Health Care," *Peoples' Weekly World*, December 12, 1998.
Heather MacDonald	"Advocates of Excuses," *New York Post*, February 1, 2002.
Myron Magnet	"More Humbug on Homelessness," *Soundings*, Winter 2000. www.city-journal.org.
Medicine & Health	"Uninsured People Get Less Care, Worse Care," May 27, 2002.
Nation	"Should America Be Measured by Its 3.5 Million Millionaires or by Its 30 Million Hungry?" December 21, 1998.
Tom Oswald	"Research Finds Poverty, Not Race, Key Factor in Breast Cancer Deaths," *MSU Today*, November 12, 2002.
Time	"Cracking Down on the Homeless: Cities Are Herding Them off the Streets but Moving a Lot Slower in Dealing with the Underlying Causes," December 20, 1999.
Viet Nam News	"Equality in Health Care a Crucial Weapon in the Fight Against Poverty," July 19, 2002. www.vietnamnews.vnagency.com.
Cheryl Wetzstein	"USDA Reports Hunger on Decline in Nation," *Washington Times*, September 8, 2000.

CHAPTER 2

What Are the Causes of Poverty in America?

Chapter Preface

With complex social problems such as poverty, distinguishing the causes of the problem from its effects can be difficult. Social workers and scientists have often debated whether ill health is a cause of poverty or one of its effects. In fact, ill health is both a cause and an effect of poverty. Researchers have been able to establish that with each step down the economic scale from rich to poor, health care becomes more expensive for the patient while health outcomes worsen. For example, many poor working families who do not qualify for government health programs such as Medicaid go to hospital emergency rooms when they need medical care. Because they are uninsured, they are completely responsible for all charges. Lack of insurance also means that they are charged a higher rate for hospital services. Thus, a single hospital visit can financially devastate an already poor family. Add lost pay for time away from a minimum wage job to attend to health problems and the case for poor health as a cause of poverty becomes stronger. With over 40 million low-income Americans lacking health insurance, many commentators believe that health care issues are central to the problem of poverty in America.

Moreover, mounting bills from catastrophic illness or injury can push even those with health insurance into poverty. In 1999 nearly half of the more than one million Americans who filed for bankruptcy did so because of medical bills or the financial effects—job or business loss—of illness or injury, according to a study conducted by Elizabeth Warren, a law professor at Harvard Law School. She maintains that this is a direct consequence of the American health care system, which requires each family to deal individually with its health problems and pay the price. "The American middle class is solid and secure and prosperous—we are unlike anything ever known in history—yet American families live just one illness or accident away from complete financial collapse," Warren argues.

Poor health causes poverty just as poverty causes poor health. In a problem as large and complex as this one, cause and effect are not only linked, they are inextricably intertwined. Authors in the following chapter debate other causes of poverty, all equally complex.

> "The only way to permanently reduce poverty . . . is to stem the longer-term trends in out-of-wedlock childbearing that have historically pushed child poverty and [welfare] caseloads up."

Illegitimacy Is a Primary Cause of Poverty

Isabel V. Sawhill

Reducing out-of-wedlock births is the single most important step in reducing poverty, argues Isabel V. Sawhill in the following viewpoint. Sawhill maintains that 32 percent of babies born in the United States are born to unmarried mothers—most of whom are young and poor and will end up on welfare. The best solution to poverty caused by illegitimacy, she contends, is counseling teens to avoid sex and pregnancy until they are married and can support their families. Isabel V. Sawhill is president of the National Campaign to Prevent Teen Pregnancy and a senior fellow at the Brookings Institution.

As you read, consider the following questions:

1. According to the author, a huge increase in out-of-wedlock births combined with what other social change have created a situation in which most children born today will spend some time in a single-parent family?
2. How did the decline in shotgun marriages affect out-of-wedlock births, in Sawhill's opinion?
3. Which group has seen the largest decline in out-of-wedlock birthrates, according to the author?

Isabel V. Sawhill, "Non-Marital Births and Child Poverty in the United States," www.brook.edu, June 29, 1999. Copyright © 1999 by The Brookings Institution Press. Reproduced by permission.

B oth as President of the National Campaign to Prevent Teen Pregnancy and as a Senior Fellow at the Brookings Institution, I have become convinced that early out-of-wedlock childbearing is bad for parents, bad for society, and especially bad for the children born into such families. . . .

Three years after the enactment of welfare reform [in 1996], the new law is being hailed as a great success. Caseloads have declined dramatically since the law was signed, and with fewer individuals to support, the states are flush with money. A strong economy interacting with tougher welfare rules and more support for the working poor is helping to turn welfare checks into paychecks. But the welfare system is like a revolving door. In good times, more people move off the rolls than come on and caseloads decline. But in bad times, exactly the reverse can occur. The only way to permanently reduce poverty and its associated expense is to stem the longer-term trends in out-of-wedlock childbearing that have historically pushed child poverty and caseloads up. Unless the states invest their surplus funds in programs aimed at preventing poverty, success may be short-lived or purchased at the expense of the children it was designed to help. If every recipient who finds a job is replaced by a younger sister ill-prepared to support a family, the immutability of the revolving door will once again prevail.

- There are many ways of preventing poverty. We could invest in early childhood education, inner city schools, or in additional supports for the working poor. But unless we can reduce out-of-wedlock pregnancies and encourage the formation of two-parent families, other efforts, by themselves, may well fail.

Much more attention needs to be given to encouraging young people to defer childbearing until they are ready to be parents. Some of the funds freed up by the drop in caseloads ought to be invested in teen pregnancy prevention programs and in reconnecting fathers with their children. In the absence of such efforts, welfare reform's current success is likely to be short-lived.

Rising divorce rates combined with a huge increase in childbearing outside of marriage have led to a situation in which most children born today will spend some time in a single parent family. And since roughly half of these single parents are poor, large numbers of children are growing up in poverty as well.

Most of the Increase in Child Poverty Can Be Explained by the Growth of Female-Headed Families

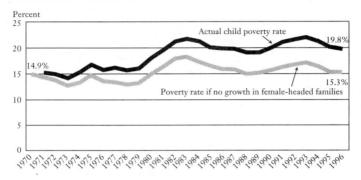

Source: U.S. Census Bureau.

The growth of female-headed families has also contributed to the growth of the welfare rolls. According to the Congressional Budget Office, welfare caseloads would have declined considerably throughout most of the 1980s if it had not been for the fact that the growth of single parent families continued to push them upwards. Moreover, this factor was more than twice as important as the economy in accounting for the roughly one million increase in the basic caseload between 1989 and 1993.

It is not just the growth of female-headed families but also shifts in the composition of the group that have contributed to greater poverty and welfare dependency. In the 1960s and 1970s, most of the growth of single parent families was caused by increases in divorce or separation. In the 1980s and 1990s, all of the increase has been driven by out-of-wedlock childbearing. Currently, 32 percent of all children in the United States and more then half in many large cities are born outside of marriage. Unmarried mothers tend to be younger and more disadvantaged than their divorced counterparts. They are overwhelmingly poor and about three-quarters of them end up on welfare.

A large fraction of babies born outside of marriage have mothers who are *not* teenagers. However, the pattern of out-of-wedlock childbearing is often established at a young age. Specifically, more than half of *first* out-of-wedlock births are to teens. So if we want to reduce such births and the welfare dependency that usually ensues, the adolescent years are a good place to start.

There are two strategies that can be used to reduce teen, out-of-wedlock births. One is to encourage marriage. The other is to discourage sex, pregnancy, and births among teens. This latter strategy has the advantage of being more consistent with the growing requirements of the economy for workers with higher levels of education and with evidence that teenage marriages are highly unstable.

Out-of-Wedlock Childbearing: Cause or Symptom of Poverty?

Some contend that many of the women who have babies as unmarried teens would have ended up poor and on welfare even if they had married and delayed childbearing. The argument is that they come from disadvantaged families and neighborhoods, have gone to poor schools, or faced other adverse influences that make having a baby at a young age as good an option as any other. There are few men with jobs for them to marry, and given their own lack of skills, welfare seems like a relatively good alternative. Moreover, earnings for less skilled men have plummeted over the past 30 years.

Although such arguments cannot be dismissed entirely, they are only a small part of the story. To begin with, the drop in marriage rates, which has been especially pronounced among African Americans, has been much larger than any economic model can explain. Second, early child bearers are much less likely to complete high school, leading directly to poor long-term employment prospects for the young women involved. The children in such families suffer even greater adverse consequences, including poorer health, less success in school, and more behavior problems. Finally, the argument that declining earnings has made marriage less viable is a curious one. Two adults can live more cheaply than one, and by pooling whatever earnings can be secured from even intermittent or low paid employment, they will be better off than a single adult living alone. These arguments are doubly true once a child enters the picture and one parent either needs to stay home or shoulder the extra expense of paying for child care.

One can grant that the earnings prospects of poorly educated, inner city residents are not good and have deteriorated in recent decades, and that better schools and more support systems for low-income working families would help. Still, early out-of-wedlock childbearing greatly compounds the problem. Even well-educated individuals in their twenties have difficulty living on one income these days, and most middle class families have two earners. Yet, for some reason, it is assumed that if the men in low-income communities can't command a decent wage, they are not marriageable. But fathers are, or should be, more than just a meal ticket. And although two minimum wage jobs will not make anyone rich, they will provide an income of about $20,000 a year, well above the poverty level for a family with two children. In short, marriage and delayed childbearing have the potential to solve a lot of problems, including assuring a better future for the next generation.

Teen Pregnancy and Out-of-Wedlock Birthrates Are High

As teen pregnancy and childbearing have become more common, they have also become more acceptable, or at least less stigmatized. A few decades ago, there were real social penalties to be paid if a girl became pregnant outside of marriage. Young girls refrained from sex for fear of becoming pregnant and being socially ostracized. Among those who did get pregnant, shotgun marriages were common. Young men had to compete for women's affections by promising marriage or at least commitment. All of this changed during the 1970s and 1980s. Contraception and abortion became much more available, women became more liberated, and sexual mores changed dramatically. A study by George Akerlof and Janet Yellen documents how the decline in shotgun marriages contributed to a rising tide of out-of-wedlock births. But this same change in sexual mores led not just to fewer marriages but also to a lot more sexual activity and a rising pregnancy rate among the nation's youth.

Teen pregnancy rates increased from the early 1970s until 1990 and have been declining since that time. The relatively modest growth . . . is the result of two offsetting trends since 1972: increased sexual activity among teens combined with greater use of contraception. If teens had not increased their use of contraception over this period, teen pregnancy rates would have soared and been almost 40 percent higher by now. On the other hand, contraceptive use did not keep pace with the greater tendency of teens to engage in sex, with the result that, up until recently, the pregnancy rate kept rising. In the war between sex and safer sex, sex won.

These increases in pregnancy rates have not always translated into higher birthrates. The greater availability of abortion after 1973 kept the teen birthrate somewhat in check. But few people, whatever their position on this difficult issue, want abortion to be the major means of preventing poverty and welfare dependency.

Teen Pregnancy and Birthrates Are Now Declining

In the 1990s, teenage sexual activity stopped increasing or even declined a bit. This combined with greater utilization of contraception among teens has caused the teen pregnancy rate to decline for the first time in decades. Teen births have fallen as well and the proportion of all children born out-of-wedlock has stabilized. The drop in birthrates among unmarried black teens is especially striking. It has declined by almost one fifth since 1991, a much sharper drop than that experienced by any other group.

What has caused this recent turnaround in sexual activity, pregnancy, and out-of-wedlock births? No one really knows but there are several possible explanations. One is fear of AIDS, which is widely suspected to be the most important reason for teens' willingness to either abstain from sex or use contraception more frequently than in the past.

Another possible explanation is welfare reform itself. Although the trends predate welfare reform, they may have gotten an extra push from the debate leading up to enactment of the new law in 1996 and the state reforms that preceded it. Most researchers don't expect welfare reform to have a big impact on out-of-wedlock childbearing. (Past studies are somewhat inconsistent, but most find that welfare has had only minor effects.) However, the new law makes welfare, and thus unwed motherhood, as a life choice much more difficult. And past research may not be a very good guide to future behavior because it has been based on variations in welfare benefits across states, not system-wide changes that are accompanied by time limits and strong moral messages that have the potential to change community norms.

Another factor that can't be dismissed is the performance of the economy over this period. The unemployment rate peaked in 1992 at 7.5 percent and has fallen sharply since. The long and very robust expansion, combined with increases in the minimum wage and in the Earned Income Tax Credit, may have helped to make work more attractive than welfare, and provided young women with more of a reason to defer childbearing. (This explanation is consistent with a surprisingly steep rise in the labor force participation of less educated single mothers since 1990.) And finally, tougher enforcement of child support laws may have made young men think twice before producing a baby. . . .

Decreasing Teen Pregnancy Will Reduce Poverty

In conclusion, reducing teen pregnancy could substantially decrease child poverty, welfare dependency, and other social ills. Although little is known with certainty about how to advance this objective, states now have the opportunity to experiment with a variety of promising approaches that are critical to the longer-term success of current welfare reform efforts. Whatever approach states choose, they should remain cognizant of the importance of strengthening the social norm that teen out-of-wedlock childbearing is—to put it most simply—wrong.

"Welfare mothers were identified . . . as the cause of everything bad, from the epidemic of drug use to the national debt to rising crime rates."

Unmarried Mothers Are Unfairly Blamed for Poverty

Susan Douglas and Meredith Michaels

Single celebrity moms and single welfare moms are two sides of the same illegitimate coin, Susan Douglas and Meredith Michaels argue in the following viewpoint. While wealthy celebrities are glorified for their single motherhood, poor women on welfare are vilified for theirs. Welfare moms are unfairly blamed for all sorts of social ills, the authors contend, because the media portray them as lazy "welfare queens" deserving nothing but scorn. In reality, Douglas and Michaels maintain, most welfare moms do the most with what they have. Susan Douglas teaches communication studies at the University of Michigan. Meredith Michaels teaches philosophy at Smith College.

As you read, consider the following questions:
1. The authors maintain that celebrity moms were perfect for the late seventies through the nineties. Why?
2. Who did the media point to as the most significant cause of America's moral decay, in the authors' opinion?
3. Most welfare mothers were portrayed as black women. If white women were shown, how were they depicted?

It's 5:22 P.M. You're in the grocery check-out line. Your three-year-old is writhing on the floor, screaming, because you have refused to buy her a Teletubby pinwheel. Your six-year-old is whining, repeatedly, in a voice that could saw through cement, "But mommy, puleeze, puleeze," because you have not bought him the latest Lunchables, which features as the four food groups: chips, a candy bar, fake cheese, and artificial coloring.

To distract yourself, and to avoid the glares of other shoppers who have already deemed you the worst mother in America, you leaf through *People* magazine. Inside, Uma Thurman gushes, "Motherhood is sexy." Moving on to *Good Housekeeping*, Vanna White says of her child, "When I hear his cry at 6:30 in the morning, I have a smile on my face, and I'm not an early riser." [Thurman and White are media celebrities.] Brought back to reality by stereophonic wailing, you feel about as sexy and euphoric as [conservative talk radio host] Rush Limbaugh in a thong.

Meanwhile, *Newsweek*, also at the check-out line, offers a different view of motherhood. In one of the many stories about welfare mothers that proliferated until "welfare reform" was passed in 1996, you meet Valerie, 27, and "the three children she has by different absentee fathers." She used to live with her mother, "who, at 42, has six grandchildren." But now Valerie resides with other families, all of whom "live side-by-side in open trash-filled apartments." Hey, maybe you're not such a failure after all.

Celebrity Moms vs. Welfare Moms

Motherhood has been one of the biggest media fixations of the past two decades. And this is what so many of us have been pulled between when we see accounts of motherhood in the media: celebrity moms who are perfect, most of them white, always rich, happy, and in control, the role models we should emulate, versus welfare mothers who are irresponsible, unmarried, usually black or Latina—as if there were no white single mothers on the dole—poor, miserable, and out of control, the bad examples we should scorn.

Beginning in the late 1970s, with the founding of *People* and *Us*, and exploding with a vengeance in the '90s with *In-*

Style, the celebrity-mom profile has spread like head lice through popular magazines, especially women's. . . .

Celebrity moms were perfect for the times. They epitomized two ideals that sat in uneasy but fruitful alliance. On the one hand, they exemplified the unbridled materialism and elitism the Reagan era had spawned [named after former president Ronald Reagan]. On the other, they represented the feminist dream of women being able to have a family and a job outside the home without being branded traitors to true womanhood. Magazine editors apparently figured they could use stars to sell magazines and to serve as role models.

Single Welfare Moms Are the Root of All Evil

But now, in the year 2000, things have gotten out of control. Celebrity moms are everywhere, beaming from the comfy serenity and perfection of their lives as they give multiple interviews about their "miracle babies," what an unadulterated joy motherhood is, and all the things they do with their kids to ensure they will be perfectly normal Nobel laureates by the age of 12. These stories are hardly reassuring. They make the rest of us feel that our own lives are, as the great seventeenth century philosopher Thomas Hobbes put it, nasty, brutish, and short. So why should we care about something so banal as the celebrity mom juggernaut? One answer is that it bulldozed through so much of American popular culture just when working mothers, single mothers, and welfare mothers were identified, especially by conservative male pundits, as the cause of everything bad, from the epidemic of drug use to the national debt to rising crime rates. Remember all the hand-wringing by George Will, William Bennett, and Allan Bloom about America's "moral decay"? The biggest culprit, of course, was the single welfare mother. These guys attacked celebrity single mothers now and then, but the mud never stuck—not even, heaven help us, on that fictional celebrity single mother Murphy Brown.[1]

As the push "to end welfare as we know it" gained momentum and reached its climax in the welfare reform of

1. Brown was a sitcom character who had an out-of-wedlock baby and managed socially and financially with few problems.

1996, the canonized celebrity mom and the demonized welfare mother became ever more potent symbols, working in powerful opposition to each other. We rarely saw these very different mothers in the same publication, or even considered them in the same breath. Celebrity moms graced the covers of magazines designed for self-realization and escape; welfare mothers were the object of endless stories in newspapers and newsmagazines and on the nightly news that focused on public policy and its relation to the tenuous state of morality in America.

But what if we put these portrayals side by side and compare what these different mothers were made to stand for? Could it be that the tsunami of celebrity-mom profiles helped, however inadvertently, to justify punitive policies toward welfare mothers and their children? While the "you can have it all" ethos of these pieces made the rest of us feel like failures as mothers, and upped the ante in the eyes of employers and coworkers about how much working mothers can handle, a little side-by-side reading also exposes some rather daunting hypocrisy. Often, one group is glamorized and the other castigated for precisely the same behavior. . . .

Welfare Moms Are the Subjects of Scrutiny

Celebrity mom profiles place us on the outside looking in; stories about welfare mothers invite us to look down from on high. Welfare mothers have not been the subject of honey-hued profiles in glossy magazines. They are not the subjects of their own lives, but objects of journalistic scrutiny. We don't hear about these women's maternal practices—what they do with their kids to nurture them, educate them, soothe them, or keep them happy. It is simply assumed that these women don't have inner lives. Emotions are not ascribed to them; we don't hear them laugh or see their eyes well up with tears. One of the most frequent verbs used to describe them is "complain," as when they complain about losing health care for their kids when they go off welfare. When they are quoted, it is not their feelings about the transformative powers of motherhood to which we are made privy. Rather, we hear their relentless complaints about "the system." In many articles about welfare, we don't hear from the mothers at all, but instead from academic experts who study them, or from politicians whose careers are devoted to bashing them. The iconography of the welfare mother is completely different, too—she's not photographed holding her child up in the air, whizzing her about. In fact, she's rarely, if ever, shown smiling at all. It's as if the photographer yelled "scowl" just before clicking the shutter.

The Media Stereotype Welfare Mothers

These mothers are shown as sphinx-like, monolithic, part of a pathetic historical pattern known, familiarly, as "the cycle of dependency." In a major article in *Newsweek* in August 1993 titled "The Endangered Family," we learned that "For many African Americans, marriage and childbearing do not go together." Not to mention the 25 percent of white women for whom they don't go together either, or the celebrity single mothers like Jodie Foster, Madonna, and Farah Fawcett.

It isn't just that the conservative right has succeeded in stereotyping welfare mothers as lazy, promiscuous parasites; the media in which these mothers appear provide no point of identification with them. At best, these mothers are pitiable. At worst, they are reprehensible opposites of the other mothers we see so much of, the new standard-bearers of ideal motherhood—the doting, conscientious celebrities for whom motherhood is a gateway to heaven. During the height of welfare bashing in the Reagan, Bush, and Clinton administrations, the stereotype of the "welfare queen" gained mythological status. But there were other, less obvious, journalistic devices that served equally well to dehumanize poor mothers and their children. Unsavory designations proliferated with a vengeance: "chronic dependents," "the chronically jobless," "welfare mothers in training," "hardcore welfare recipients," "never-married mothers," "welfare careerists," and "welfare recidivists" became characters in a distinctly American political melodrama. Poor women weren't individuals; instead their life stories became case-studies of moral decay, giving substance to the inevitable barrage of statistics peppering the media's presentation of "Life on the Dole." In publications everywhere, we met the poster mother for welfare reform. She only had a first name, she lived in the urban decay of New York, Chicago, or Detroit, she was not married, she had a pile of kids each with a different absent father, and she spent her day painting her nails, smoking cigarettes, and feeding Pepsi to her baby.

More Whites than African Americans Are on Welfare

As sociologists have pointed out, even though there consistently have been more white people than black on welfare, the news media began, in the mid-1960s, to rely almost exclusively on pictures of African Americans to illustrate stories about welfare, reinforcing the stereotype that most welfare recipients are black. Occasionally readers are introduced to the runner-up in the poster competition: the white welfare mother, whose story varies only in that she lives in a trailer in some godforsaken place we have never heard of and is really, really fat.

A Woman's Work in the Home Has No Value

Most state administrators, politicians, journalists, and researchers see the work of taking care of children as a cost of welfare-to-work, but not as an important and valuable family activity. Devaluing women's unpaid work in the home is clearly evident in studies of welfare reform. Typically, researchers compare welfare families' and employed families' material well-being without imputing any value to women's time. In short, the value of women's unpaid labor in the home when she is receiving welfare is zero. As a policy, welfare-to-work fails to grapple with the fact that adults responsible for children cannot (and probably should not) put their jobs—especially low-wage ones—before the needs of their children.

Randy Albelda, *Dollars and Sense*, September/October 2000.

For example, in a 1995 edition of CBS's *48 Hours*, titled "The Rage Over Welfare," we met two overweight white women who live on welfare in New Hampshire. The very first shots—just to let us know the kind of lazy, selfish mothers we are in for—are close-ups of hands shuffling a deck of playing cards and, next, a mom lighting a cigarette. The white male journalist badgers one of the women, who says she can't work because she has epilepsy and arthritis in both knees. "People with epilepsy work. People with bad knees work. People do," he scolds. As she answers, "I don't know what kind of a job I could find," the camera again cuts to her hands shuffling the cards, suggesting, perhaps, a bright future in the casino industry if she'd only apply herself.

Or there's Denise B., one of the "True Faces of Welfare," age 29, with five daughters, from ages one to 13. "All, after the first, were conceived on welfare—conceived perhaps deliberately," *Reader's Digest* sniffs, conjuring up the image of Denise doing some quick math calculations, saying to herself, Oh boy, an extra 60 bucks a month, and then running out to find someone to get her pregnant. The other thing we learn about Denise is that she's a leech. Why not get a job, even though she has toddlers? Because she's lazy. "To get a good job, she would first have to go to school, then earn her way up to a high salary," *Reader's Digest* reminds us, and then lets the ingrate, Denise, speak. "'That's going to take time,' she says, 'It's a lot of work and I ain't guaranteed to get nothing.'" What we learn of Denise's inner life is that she's a calculating cynic. Her kids don't make her feel like every day is Christmas; no, we're supposed to think she uses her kids to get something for nothing.

Celebrity Mom's Sexuality Is Good—Welfare Mom's Sexuality Is Bad

Even the *New York Times*'s Jason De Parle, one of the more sympathetic white male journalists to cover welfare, gets blinded by class privilege. Roslyn Hale, he wrote in 1994, who had been trying to get off welfare, had a succession of jobs that "alternatively invite and discourage public sympathy." She had worked as a maid and as a clerk in a convenience store during the overnight shift when drunks came in and threatened her with a knife. Hale "blames economics for her problems," De Parle reports, since these were crappy jobs that paid only minimum wage. "And sometimes she blames herself. 'I have an attitude,' she admitted." Hello? What middle-class woman would not have "an attitude" after having been threatened at knifepoint or being expected to be grateful for such jobs? In the *Boston Globe*'s "Welfare

Reform Through a Child's Eyes" we see little Alicia, who now has a room of her own, Barbies, four kittens, and a ferret because her mother got a job. But although this story appears to be through the child's eyes (never the mother's), it's actually through the judgmental eyes of the press. Sure, the mom has quit drinking, quit crack, and is now working at a nursing center. But the apartment is "suffused with the aroma of animal droppings and her mother's cigarette smoke." Presumably everyone but welfare mothers and former welfare mothers knows how to make their litter boxes smell like gardenias. One of the sentences most commonly used to characterize the welfare mother is "Tanya, who has _____ children by _____ different men . . ." (you fill in the blanks). Their lives are reduced to the number of successful impregnations by multiple partners—like zoo animals, but unlike [movie star] Christie Brinkley, although she has exactly the same reproductive M.O. And while the celebrity magazines gush that Christie . . . [is] sexier than ever, a welfare mother's sexuality is depicted as her downfall.

The Media Make It Easy to Resent Welfare Recipients

In the last three years, we've seen the dismantling of the nation's welfare system. Meanwhile, the resentment over the ridiculous standards we're supposed to meet is rising. Sure, many of us ridicule these preposterous portraits of celebrity mom-dom, and we gloated when the monumentally self-righteous "I read the Bible to Cody" Kathie Lee Gifford [television personality] got her various comeuppances. But the problem is bigger than that: the standards set by celebrity motherhood as touted by the media, with their powerful emphasis on individual will, choice, and responsibility, severely undercut sympathy for poor mothers and their children. Both media characterizations have made it easier for middle-class and upper-middle-class women—especially working women facing speed-ups at work and a decline in leisure time—to resent welfare mothers instead of identifying with them and their struggles.

"Marijuana and cocaine use significantly increase the probability of being poor."

Substance Abuse Causes Poverty

Robert Kaestner

In the following viewpoint, Robert Kaestner argues that the physiological effects of substance abuse—especially chronic abuse—reduces users' physical and mental abilities, which lowers productivity, reduces earnings, and increases the likelihood of poverty. Moreover, Kaestner maintains that patterns of substance abuse are established at an early age and impact other life decisions affecting poverty, such as whether or not to stay in school. Robert Kaestner is a professor in the school of public affairs and department of economics at Baruch College, City University of New York, and a research associate at the National Bureau of Economic Research.

As you read, consider the following questions:
1. In Kaestner's opinion, what important contribution can social science make?
2. According to the author, how does family composition affect poverty?
3. How is drug use linked to poverty through its effect on marriage and fertility, in Kaestner's opinion?

Robert Kaestner, "Does Drug Use Cause Poverty?" *The Economic Analysis of Substance Use and Abuse*, edited by Frank J. Chaloupka, Michael Grossman, Warren K. Bickel, and Henry Saffer. Chicago: University of Chicago Press, 1999.

To a majority of Americans, illicit drug use and poverty go hand-in-hand. Poverty is concentrated in inner-city neighborhoods that are also characterized by high rates of drug use and drug dealing activity. Similarly, the homeless population primarily found in cities consists of a high proportion of drug users. On a more personal level, drug use of acquaintances, friends and family members often becomes known only at a time of crisis when the drug using individual has experienced some type of significant personal setback, often characterized by a worsening economic position. Thus, the public has a significant amount of empirical evidence, some anecdotal and some systematic, that links drug use and poverty. Furthermore, based on the public's support and willingness to pay for anti-drug programs, it would appear that there is a widespread belief that drug use causes many negative social and economic outcomes, including poverty.

An important contribution of social science is to validate or refute conventional wisdom. In this case, the relevant question is whether drug use really does cause poverty. There has been a substantial amount of prior research on this issue, although not always directly focused on poverty. For example, there have been several studies of the effects of drug use on various determinants of poverty: wages, labor supply, marital status, out-of-wedlock birth, and welfare participation. Surprisingly, those studies have presented only limited evidence suggesting that drug use is a cause of poverty. For example, past research has shown that drug use has relatively few adverse effects on wages and employment, two major determinants of poverty. In contrast, studies examining the effect of drug use on family composition and fertility document strong positive associations between drug use and marital delay, marital dissolution, and out-of-wedlock birth. Thus, the question of whether drug use causes poverty is unresolved, and it remains an important public issue. Indeed, the government spends considerable sums of money to eradicate drug use, and part of the justification for that spending is the supposedly adverse effects of drug use on economic well being.

The purpose of this paper is to directly examine the effect of drug use on poverty, as opposed to the effect of drug use on the determinants of poverty. The main objective of the paper is to provide descriptive empirical information about the relationship between drug use and poverty, and to explore, in a preliminary fashion, the question of whether drug use causes poverty. Toward this end, I present the results of both descriptive and multivariate analyses of the relationship between drug use and poverty for two national samples of young adults. One sample is drawn from the National Household Survey of Drug Abuse (NHSDA), and the other from the National Longitudinal Survey of Youth (NLSY). The results of the analysis indicate that for both samples, drug use is associated with greater poverty.

Figure 1 provides a simple overview of the various ways that drug use may affect poverty. In Figure 1, poverty is primarily determined by labor market outcomes, but is also affected by family composition. Family composition affects poverty by altering family size, and sources and quantity of non-earned income. Labor market outcomes are determined by a person's human capital, which in this case is summa-

Figure 1. The Ways Drug Use May Affect Poverty

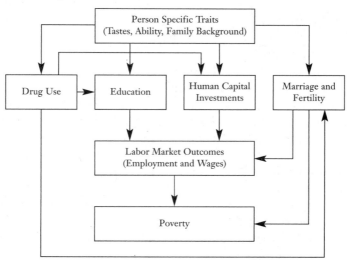

Robert Kaestner, National Bureau of Economic Research Working Paper, February 1998.

rized by a person's level of education and other human capital investments (e.g., training and health). Labor market outcomes may also be affected by family composition. For example, single-parents may not be able to work as many hours as childless individuals. Drug use and poverty are related because drug use affects the determinants of poverty: education, human capital investments, marriage and fertility. Finally, person specific factors such as ability, preferences and family background affect drug use as well as educational achievement, skill accumulation, marriage and fertility.

Drug Use Reduces Physical and Mental Abilities

For the most part, the implied relationships in Figure 1 are obvious and consistent with intuition. The prime example of this statement being the effect of drug use on human capital. The physiological effects of drug use, particularly those related to chronic drug use, suggest that drugs reduce physical and cognitive abilities. Consequently, drug use is expected to lower productivity, reduce earnings, and result in an increased likelihood of poverty. Similarly, drug use may adversely affect educational achievement, or attainment, and hence lower earnings and increase poverty. Somewhat less obvious, however, are the ways in which drug use may affect poverty through its effect on marriage and fertility. There are, however, several reasons why drug use may affect marriage and fertility. Drug use may affect a person's ability to use contraception, or their judgment related to contraception use, and lead to more out-of-wedlock births. Or drug use may cause more marital strife and lead to marital dissolution. Finally, drug use may affect the likelihood of finding a spouse because of preferences (e.g., stigma) regarding persons who use drugs. All of these potential consequences of drug use would tend to increase poverty. . . .

Figure 1 also illustrates the important part that ability, preferences and family background may have in determining both poverty and drug use. For example, a person with a high rate of time preference is more likely to use drugs, make fewer human capital investments, and experience more poverty than an otherwise similar person with a lower rate of time preference. . . .

One piece of evidence supporting the causal model of Figure 1, is that initiation of drug use usually occurs prior to marriage, child bearing, and many human capital investments. For example, among those who report some prior marijuana use, 75 percent had first used marijuana by age 18, and 95 percent had first used marijuana by age 21. For cocaine, the age of initiation is somewhat higher, but even in this case, 50 percent of all individuals reporting some prior use, also report that they had first used cocaine by age 19; and 75 percent of this group report first using cocaine by age 22. All of these figures come from the 1994 NHSDA and pertain to a sample of adults between the ages of 18 and 40. These relatively early ages of initiation are consistent with the specification of the causal model in Figure 1. Patterns of drug use and risk of drug use are established at relatively early ages, prior to the time of most investments in human capital and before marriage. Moreover, models of rational addiction such as that of Becker and Murphy (1988) would suggest that drug users are forward looking, and that these early consumption choices establish a pattern of use that should be little affected by planned investments in education and human capital. Indeed, early consumption choices are made with full knowledge regarding expected future choices of drug use, education, marriage, fertility and other human capital investments. . . .

In this paper, I have obtained a variety of estimates of the effect of marijuana and cocaine use on poverty using two national samples of young adults. A large preponderance of the estimates indicated that marijuana and cocaine use significantly increase the probability of being poor. Drug users had lower family incomes, and were more likely to participate in public assistance programs than non-users. In some cases, estimates were quite large implying 50 percent or more increases in the rate of poverty, as measured in this paper. These results indicate that drug use is a serious problem, and suggest that public policies focusing on reducing drug use would have some positive economic effects on people's lives.

"If all welfare recipients were to stop using illicit drugs, the size of the welfare population would show little decline."

The Link Between Substance Abuse and Poverty Has Been Exaggerated

Joint Center for Poverty Research

In the following viewpoint, the editors at the Joint Center for Poverty Research (JCPR) argue that the prevalence of substance use and dependence among welfare recipients is overstated. Only one-fifth of recipients used some illicit drug during the last year, the center contends. Moreover, drug use among recipients declined from approximately 30 percent in 1990 to 21 percent in 1998. The editors maintain that poor education, lack of transportation, and physical and mental health problems are more common causes of poverty than substance abuse. The JCPR is a national academic research center that explores the meaning of poverty in America.

As you read, consider the following questions:
1. How do the trends in drug use for welfare recipients compare to those of nonrecipients, as reported by the center?
2. According to the center, what percentage of Women's Employment Study respondents were drug dependent?
3. What does the organization argue should be done with welfare recipients who experience drug use disorders?

Harold A. Pollack, Sheldon Danziger, Kristin Seefeldt, and Rukmalie Jayakody, "Substance Use and Dependence Among Welfare Recipients," www.jcpr.org, January 22, 2002. Copyright © 2002 by the Joint Center for Poverty Research. Reproduced by permission.

As welfare caseloads shrink in response to reforms in 1996, those remaining on the rolls are often those with many barriers to working. Many researchers and program administrators suggest that alcohol and drug abuse is widespread among welfare recipients and an important barrier to self-sufficiency.

Harold Pollack and colleagues, in their Joint Center for Poverty Research (JCPR) working paper, "Substance Use Among Welfare Recipients: Trends and Policy Responses," find that substance dependence and use are less a problem among welfare recipients than the general public assumes. They find that approximately 20% of the Temporary Assistance for Needy Families (TANF) caseload in 1998 used drugs or alcohol, and that many fewer were dependent on alcohol or drugs. Although it is true that drug use is greater among welfare recipients than among the general population, the prevalence of drug use declined during the 1990s among welfare recipients and nonrecipients alike.

Drug Use Common Among TANF Recipients

Based on data from National Household Survey of Drug Abuse (NHSDA) from 1990–1998, the authors find that the prevalence of drug use among welfare recipients at any time during the year declined from approximately 30% in 1990 to approximately 21% in 1998. Contrary to the beliefs of many policymakers and policy advocates, illicit drug use was less prevalent at the end of the 1990s than at the beginning of the decade, even though the welfare caseload was cut roughly in half nationwide during that timespan.

Illicit drug use remains more common among welfare recipients than nonrecipients; however, trends within the two groups are similar. Between 1990 and 1998, illicit drug use during the previous year fell from 29.8% to 21.3% among welfare recipients and from 22.7% to 12.5% among unmarried women aged 18–54 who did not receive cash assistance.

The authors find the more serious drug dependence to be about twice as common among TANF recipients than nonrecipients. Approximately 4.5% of recipients met diagnostic screening criteria for dependence, while 2.1% of nonrecipients met the same criteria. The difference is statistically significant. The authors find suggestive, but statistically insignificant, differences in the prevalence of alcohol dependence between recipients and nonrecipients. Approximately 7.5% of welfare recipients met criteria for alcohol dependence compared with 4.6% of nonrecipients.

Drug Dependence Is Rare

The NHSDA data available to the study team could only track drug use differences between welfare recipients and nonrecipients through 1998. The authors relied on longitudinal data from the Michigan Women's Employment Study (WES) to extend trends through late 1999.

Drug Trade, Not Use, High in Poor Areas

Although residents of the poorest US neighborhoods are likely to see illegal drug sales in plain view, they are no more likely to abuse drugs than people in more affluent neighborhoods, researchers report.

American Journal of Public Health, December 6, 2001.

The WES interviewed women in one urban Michigan county in three waves, in late 1997, 1998, and 1999. Because Michigan allows women to receive cash assistance for an interim period while working, WES data allowed further comparisons of substance use and dependence by work status and by continued receipt of TANF.

Trends in drug use and dependence in the first three WES waves were similar to those of the NHSDA. Drug dependence was rare; 3.2% of WES respondents met the criteria. As with the NHSDA, drug dependence was higher among TANF recipients, working or not, than among nonrecipients. Drug dependence was much more common among nonworking TANF recipients than among those combining work and welfare. About 1% of combiners were considered drug-dependent compared with 7.5% of those not working.

Prevalence of Substance Abuse Overstated

The prevalence of substance use and dependence among welfare recipients is easily overstated. Approximately one-fifth of recipients reported using some illicit drugs during the last year [2001]. Poor education, lack of transportation, physical and mental health problems, and many other difficulties are more common than substance use disorders. If all welfare recipients were to stop using illicit drugs, the size of the welfare population would show little decline.

However, for those who are dependent on drugs or alcohol, it appears to be a barrier to employment, given that more alcohol- or drug-dependent women were not working. Currently, fewer than 5% of recipients are referred for treatment. Further, the need for services and treatment appears high within identifiable groups, such as sanctioned recipients. In one county in New Jersey, for example, nearly half of sanctioned recipients met criteria for a substance use disorder.

These findings also highlight the importance of screening, assessment, and appropriate services for welfare recipients who experience drug use disorders. Simply removing drug-dependent women from the welfare rolls may only aggravate the difficulties faced by families. A cautionary tale is provided by the abrupt reform of the "drug and alcohol addiction" component of federal disability programs. A survey of former Supplemental Security Income recipients who lost benefits owing to this policy change found that about half were earning less than $500 a month one year after losing benefits.

"Dependency cannot be overcome by income transfers, but it can be overcome by the promotion of the habits or virtues that foster self-reliance."

A Lack of Individual Responsibility Causes Poverty

Joel Schwartz

What the poor need most, Joel Schwartz argues in the following viewpoint, is to take responsibility for themselves. The best antipoverty program, he contends, is one that encourages the poor to become thrifty and diligent. Government programs such as Individual Development Accounts that encourage long-term saving and provide matching funds and financial education are preferable to programs that simply hand out checks, he asserts. Furthermore, Schwartz maintains that if society wants to reduce poverty, nonpoor individuals should model the virtues expected of the poor. Joel Schwartz is a contributing editor to *Philanthropy* and author of *Fighting Poverty with Virtue: Moral Reform and America's Urban Poor, 1825–2000*.

As you read, consider the following questions:
1. What is the purpose of subsidizing self-reliance, according to Schwartz?
2. Why does the author maintain that while Individual Development Accounts are an excellent tool to teach the virtue of saving, they won't work for everyone?
3. What are two of the virtues espoused by moral reformers of the nineteenth century, according to Schwartz?

For much of the twentieth century, it was generally assumed that to help the poor, one must give them money, because that was what they chiefly needed. Today a new consensus has arisen on helping the poor. In the words of a 1987 manifesto (published by the American Enterprise Institute) that accurately forecasted the evolution of welfare policy, "low income is in a sense the least of [the] problems" of many among the poor, for whom "a failure to take responsibility for themselves and for their actions is at the core." While it is easy to transfer money, "to overcome behavioral dependency requires a much more human, complex, and difficult engagement."

Dependency cannot be overcome by income transfers, but it can be overcome by the promotion of the habits or virtues that foster self-reliance. The "difficult engagement" of contemporary anti-poverty policy lies in its attempt to encourage the virtues of thrift and diligence.

To some extent, the effort to encourage these virtues is self-contradictory, because it amounts to subsidizing self-reliance. For example, if a welfare mother eager to work is given a subsidy to help pay for transportation to her job (or for child care), is she self-reliant (because she is working) or dependent (because her work-related expenses are subsidized)?

The obvious answer is, both. Policies designed to promote thrift and diligence recognize that self-reliance and dependence are not all-or-nothing propositions. Subsidies for transportation and child care aim to wean the poor from absolute and prolonged dependency. They offer an incentive, or at least reduce a disincentive, in the hope of promoting virtuous behavior and assisting the poor in gradual steps to more and more self-reliance.

The Poor Should Be Encouraged to Save

Encouraging the virtue of thrift certainly helps the poor to help themselves. Some of the reforms in this area reverse long-time welfare policies. For example, in the pre-reform welfare system persons who received Aid to Families with Dependent Children routinely had their assets seized if they saved more than $1,000. This strongly discouraged saving among the poor. A 1997 survey of credit union members with low incomes found that 49 percent of the recipients of public assistance among them agreed that "I would save more, but the government would cut my benefits if I did."

The 1996 welfare reform law permitted states to raise these limits, in order to reduce welfare recipients' disincentive to save. As of now, almost all states have increased asset limits.

In addition to removing disincentives to saving, the movement to encourage thrift among the poor also incorporates efforts to reward poor people who do save. "Typically, the poor have been told they should work hard and save more," observes Michael Sherraden, the leading proponent of policies designed to increase the savings of poor Americans, "but historically, there have been few programs or incentives to encourage them to do it."

How might the poor be encouraged to save? Sherraden advocates the creation of Individual Development Accounts or IDAs, which are modeled on the IRAs popular with the middle class. In an IDA, deposited funds (and the earnings they accrue) are either tax-exempt or tax-deferred. The funds cannot be withdrawn to pay for immediate consumption, but instead can be used only for specific purposes that require long-term saving—for example, purchasing a first home, paying for education or job training, or opening a small business. For poor people, the government matches any contributions made to an IDA account, and requires recipients of IDA funds to attend financial education classes.

Twenty-Nine States Have Created IDAs

The states were given power to create IDA programs as part of the 1996 welfare reform bill. As of the end 2000, 29 states had done so. Foundations have also been interested in experimenting with IDAs. In 1997, the Downpayments on the American Dream Policy Demonstration was launched with a six-year, $8 million grant from the Ford, Joyce, and Charles Stewart Mott Foundations, and an additional $4 million from local partners, such as churches, corporations, and banks. The project has set up about 2,000 IDAs in 13 cities.

Although IDAs promise to do much good by encouraging the discipline of saving among the poor, they are not a panacea. Some poor people don't make enough money to save, and others lack the capacity for self-denial. But as Tom Riley observes in *Philanthropy*, "by requiring participants to make a very real (if short-term) sacrifice, and by insisting on the financial education component, IDAs can, by design, sort out the people that they *can* help from those that they can't."

The virtue of diligence—sticking to one's work—is, of course, the central premise of the nation's reformed welfare system. As *New York Times* reporter Jason DeParle put it in 1997, "If the emerging programs share a unifying theme, it can be summarized in a word: *work*. States are demanding that recipients find it faster, keep it longer, and perform it as a condition of aid. Most states regard even a low-paying, dead-end job as preferable to the education and training programs they offered in the past."

As is well known, this emphasis on work has been accompanied by a notable drop in the welfare rolls. Admittedly, even proponents of welfare reform recognize that in some respects it is still too early to celebrate its unequivocal triumph. A 1998 General Accounting Office report—while quite supportive of the reform—nevertheless makes clear that many important questions remain unanswered: We don't yet know the extent to which families who have left welfare will later return to it. We don't yet know how economically stable families are after leaving welfare. We don't yet know what happens to children who lose assistance because their families fail to comply with the new requirements of welfare programs. We don't know how the welfare rolls will be affected by a weak economy.

Some Welfare Recipients Are Unemployable

Still, one pessimistic reading of the evidence is misguided, namely, that welfare rolls have dropped only because the most easily employable "cream" of the welfare population found jobs. The real test, it is argued, won't come until later, when attempts are made to find jobs for hard-core recipients like the homeless, the addicted, the battered, the disturbed, the illiterate, and the criminal, who perhaps composed as much as one-third of the original caseload.

Now common sense certainly suggests that those who have left the welfare rolls already are the ones who are comparatively employable, and that those who remain on the rolls are less so. But on another level, this line of argument is seriously wrongheaded: it implies that what was in fact a scandal of the old system—the dependency, in some cases the prolonged dependency, of employable persons—actually points to a failing of the new system.

Hard Work Can End Poverty

Most Americans believe that if one works hard, one should not be poor. Yet the working poor constitute one of the fastest-growing segments of the impoverished population, and their growth is expected to continue. According to the official government definition of poverty, which compares family income to a minimum standard of living, the working poor number nine million. This number doubles, however, when measures of poverty are used that more closely reflect what most Americans think is necessary to live on.

Marlene Kim, *Challenge*, May/June 1998.

The welfare rolls may currently include a significant number of people who are unemployable. Nevertheless, the current employment of many past recipients is a *triumph* of welfare reform today, not an indication of its likely failure tomorrow. Much if not all of the "cream" of the welfare population should not have been on welfare in the first place, and a system that encouraged their dependency must have been gravely flawed, while one that liberates them from dependency deserves celebration.

Yes, the hiring of employable welfare recipients was obviously helped along by the great economic prosperity of the 1990s. But prosperity can't have reduced the rolls all by itself. As Michael Barone of *U.S. News & World Report* observes, the rolls surged upwards during the 1960s, despite considerable economic expansion and job creation. So the recent decline in the number of welfare recipients is due in part to an increased acknowledgment of the moral dangers of prolonged dependency. This altered moral understanding returns us to something like the perspective of the moral reformers of the nineteenth century—insightful advocates of virtues like diligence and thrift—whose story I relate in my new book, *Fighting Poverty with Virtue*.

Self-Reliance Is the Goal of Welfare Reform

The goal of welfare reform rightly understood is ultimately less economic (cutting welfare costs) than moral (encouraging self-reliance, even if it's only partial, subsidized self-reliance). As author Daniel Casse explains, it's wrong to think the welfare debate "was ever about the amount of money the country was spending." If the billions of tax dollars spent in recent decades "had gone into a poverty assistance program that had actually helped to foster stable families, safe and clean public housing, higher achievement in education, and a reduction in illegimate births, no one would ever have complained about a welfare 'crisis' in the first place." Instead of focusing on the non-problem of money, the current reform forces "both federal and state governments to take seriously the idea that welfare policy can deter, or encourage, behavior."

In different and in some respects contradictory ways, public policy and the charitable practice of faith-based organizations are already doing much to encourage the poor to fight poverty with virtue. Nevertheless, the promotion of virtue is not exclusively—perhaps not even primarily—a matter for public policy and charity. To some extent it may be easier to encourage virtues like diligence and thrift (and sobriety and familial responsibility) by means of personal example than by government edict. If we want to encourage the poor to practice these virtues (as we should and must), it would be no small thing for us to act as if we believed in them by practicing them ourselves.

"What the federal government says is adequate falls far short of what families really need."

A Lack of Opportunities Causes Poverty

Ellen Mutari

Most poor families lack the educational and earning opportunities required to become self-sufficient, Ellen Mutari argues in the following viewpoint. Using *The Self-Sufficiency Standard for the City of New York* as an example, she maintains that with only low-paying jobs available to them, poor families cannot bridge the gap between what they can earn and what they need to live. Even earnings above the official poverty line fall short of meeting the needs of a single parent with two children, Mutari contends. Ellen Mutari teaches qualitative reasoning at Richard Stockton College and is a *Dollars and Sense* associate.

As you read, consider the following questions:

1. What factors does *The Self-Sufficiency Standard for the City of New York* take into account, according to the author?
2. Ellen Mutari maintains that the federal government's original calculation of poverty levels was based on the cost of what item?
3. What does the author argue will help poor people meet the goal of self-sufficiency?

Ellen Mutari, "Self-Sufficiency: An Elusive Goal," *Dollars and Sense*, July 2001, p. 42. Copyright © 2001 by *Dollars and Sense*, a progressive economics magazine. www.dollarsandsense.org. Reproduced by permission.

"I wouldn't say I'm economically self-sufficient yet," says one participant in a welfare-to-work job training program sponsored by the Women's Center for Education and Career Advancement (WCECA) in New York City. That's the point, she says, where she won't have to worry about how to pay the light bill, or how to meet her family's health care needs: "Not that you have a lot of money, but you're not worried about how your kid is going to get that next pair of shoes."

When Congress passed the Personal Responsibility and Work Opportunity Reconciliation (or "welfare reform") Act of 1997, self-sufficiency was one of the stated goals. But what kind of income does a single mother actually need to earn in order to be "self-sufficient," that is, to support a family without relying on government programs or private charity? And according to this definition of self-sufficiency, is it possible for her—or anyone else, for that matter—to be self-sufficient at all?

The Federal Poverty Line Is Set Too Low

A recent WCECA study by researcher Diana Pearce, with Jennifer Brooks, offers one answer to these questions. In their 2000 report, *The Self-Sufficiency Standard for the City of New York*, the authors estimated the amount of income required—for families in New York City's five boroughs—to adequately meet basic needs without public or private assistance. The estimates take into account variations in family size, the age of family members, and where families live. But one thing is clear: What the federal government says is adequate falls far short of what families really need.

For example, Pearce and Brooks found that a single parent living in the Bronx with two children, one in school and one in daycare, would need a gross income of $3,684 per month (or $44,208 per year) to meet basic needs. Even working full time, the parent would have to earn $20.93 per hour—much more than the typical entry-level wage for someone without specialized skills.

Let's take a look at this family's monthly budget (see Figure 1). Child care, the most expensive component, costs $1,234, or one-third of the total budget. Housing ($740 including utilities) comes next, accounting for another one-fifth. Transportation costs are a small portion of the budget because New Yorkers have access to extensive public transportation. (For families in areas where a car is needed to get to and from work, transportation costs would be much higher.) Health care costs make up only 8% ($294), because Pearce and Brooks assumed that the family was covered by employer-sponsored health insurance. (They based their calculation on the cost of the least expensive health maintenance organization in Bronx County.) Of course, many low-wage jobs do not provide health insurance, so working poor families are often forced to choose between health care and other necessities.

Original Poverty Formula Was Set in 1960

This example shows that the federal government's method of calculating poverty levels is deeply flawed. Each year, the government publishes poverty lines for families of different sizes. During the 1960s, Mollie Orshansky, a researcher in the Social Security Administration, developed the methodology that the government uses to make its calculations. Orshansky put together two pieces of information. First, the U.S. Department of Agriculture estimated that, in the 1950s, moderate-income families spent one-third of their earnings on food. Second, the agency developed a series of food plans designed to provide the minimum calories necessary for families to survive. Orshansky selected the "economy" food plan and multiplied its cost by three. This established the threshold that is now the federal poverty line. (The government adjusts the threshold by number and age of family members.) Except for taking into account the average increase in consumer prices, the government makes no other modifications to the original formula.

The Orshansky method introduces a number of problems. First, since the 1950s, the cost of most items in a family's budget—such as housing, health care, and transportation—has risen much faster than the cost of food. For example, food comprises only about an eighth of the Bronx family's budget (see Figure 1). (This means that, if we use Orshansky's method, we would have to calculate the poverty line at eight times the cost of food.) Another problem is that the original

Figure 1. Percentage of Income Needed to Meet Basic Needs, 2000

Based on the Self-Sufficiency Standard for a Family with One Parent, One Preschool-Age Child and One School-Age Child in Monroe County, NY (Rochester)

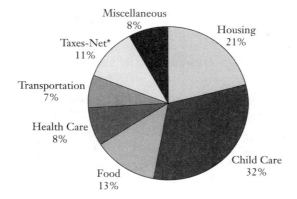

*Note: Percentages include the net effect of taxes and tax credits. Thus, the percentage of income needed for taxes is actually 17%, but with tax credits, the amount owed in taxes is reduced to 11%.

food budgets were designed only for short-term emergencies, not for ongoing nutritional needs. Finally, Orshansky's budgets did not consider the cost of child care, because they assumed that preschoolers were cared for at home.

Work Is Not Enough

When we look at other benchmarks, these problems are even more glaring. Consider the example of a single-parent family with two children, living in the borough of Queens. To be truly self-sufficient, the family would need a gross annual income of $46,836. But the federal poverty line for this family is only $14,150. And welfare benefits under the Temporary Assistance to Needy Families (TANF) program, combined with food stamps, do not even bring this family up to the federally defined poverty line! The total welfare grant package in New York City is less than one-fourth of the self-sufficiency standard.

What about work instead of welfare? A full-time minimum-wage job, paying $16,478 per year, would lift the Queens family above the federally defined poverty line. As a result, some policy makers claim that welfare-to-work is a successful strategy. But barely squeaking above the federally established poverty line is not the same as not living in poverty. When we compare minimum-wage earnings to the self-sufficiency standard, we can see that a huge gap remains. Work, in itself, is clearly not enough.

Earning Opportunities Must Be Improved

For Pearce and Brooks, the self-sufficiency standard, not the poverty line, should be the standard for measuring economic progress. How can families achieve this goal? The authors propose better access to training, education, and nontraditional jobs for women; labor market reforms such as increasing the minimum wage and passing living wage laws; and the elimination of gender and race discrimination in employment and earnings. They also call on private employers to offer health care coverage in more jobs, and they recommend improved efforts to collect child support from non-custodial parents.

At the same time, the authors call for more publicly financed support services, including targeted public subsidies for child care, housing, and children's health care, as well as larger TANF grants. These subsidies, Pearce and Brooks stress, are the key to helping families achieve economic stability and security "without scrimping on nutrition, living in overcrowded or substandard housing, or using inadequate child care."

But doesn't "self-sufficiency" mean getting by without government assistance? Pearce and Brooks portray public subsidies as a temporary solution—just until low-income families can earn enough to survive on their own. According to their definition of self-sufficiency, however, no one in the United Stares is truly self-sufficient. Just as middle-class families rely on federal transportation subsidies, federal highway spending, and mortgage interest deductions, low-income families depend on public subsidies for basic needs. There's no reason to expect poor women to be self-sufficient when no one else is expected to meet that goal.

To date, researchers have calculated self-sufficiency standards for 13 different cities and localities, including Boston, Chicago, Philadelphia, and Washington, D.C. In some of these places, the cost of living is much lower than in New York. But even in those cities, the amount of income needed to be truly self-sufficient is beyond the grasp of many families, especially those headed by single women. Better jobs and higher wages will help, but expanded public subsidies are vital.

*"To address seriously the segregation and
poverty that persist in urban America, we
must . . . educate consumers about . . .
money management and providers of
financial services about lingering
discrimination."*

Housing Discrimination Causes Poverty

Gregory D. Squires

While "neighborhood improvement associations" no longer blatantly exclude blacks from certain areas, Gregory D. Squires argues in the following viewpoint that the discriminatory practices of mortgage lenders and property insurers have perpetuated geographic segregation and poverty in American cities. Squires contends that discrimination in housing is the result of persistent prejudicial practices within the industry. As long as these practices exist, blacks and other minorities will be denied the economic benefits of home ownership, he asserts. Gregory D. Squires is a professor of sociology and faculty member of the urban studies program at the University of Wisconsin at Milwaukee.

As you read, consider the following questions:
1. According to Gregory D. Squires, what effect did Federal Housing Administration adviser Homer Hoyt maintain blacks and Mexicans had on property values?
2. How has the federal government reinforced dual housing markets, in the author's opinion?
3. What is paired testing, as related by Squires?

Gregory D. Squires, "The Indelible Color Line," *The American Prospect*, vol. 10, January 1, 1999–February 1, 1999, p. 67. Copyright © 1999 by *The American Prospect*. Reproduced by permission.

Though overt racism has diminished greatly over the last 30 years, most American cities remain deeply segregated. A host of other problems, such as the lack of both public services and private enterprise in inner-city black neighborhoods, have persisted in part because of this segregation. The challenge today is no longer to thwart individual white racists or, certainly, the patent discrimination of the old "neighborhood improvement associations," which flatly excluded blacks. Rather we must address the legacy of nearly a century of institutional practices that embedded racial and ethnic ghettos deep in our urban demography. Specifically, the practices of mortgage lenders and property insurers may have done more to shape housing patterns than bald racism ever did.

Underwriting Discrimination

Real estate agents and federal housing officials long listened to sociologist and Federal Housing Administration (FHA) advisor Homer Hoyt, who concluded in 1933 that blacks and Mexicans had a very detrimental effect on property values. In its 1939 Underwriting Manual the FHA warned of "inharmonious racial groups" and concluded that "if a neighborhood is to retain stability, it is necessary that properties shall continue to be occupied by the same social and racial classes." Until the 1960s the FHA insured the financing of many homes in white suburban areas while providing virtually no mortgage insurance in the urban markets where minorities lived. Similarly, until the 1950s the National Association of Realtors officially "steered" clients into certain neighborhoods according to race, advising that "a realtor should never be instrumental in introducing into a neighborhood a character of property or occupancy, members of any race or nationality whose presence will clearly be detrimental to property values in the neighborhood." Racially restrictive covenants were actually enforced by the courts until the Supreme Court declared them to be "unenforceable as law and contrary to public policy" in its decision in *Shelley v. Kraemer*, in 1948.

But such covenants have persisted in practice even after they were officially declared illegal. In 1989, Urban Institute researchers found that racial steering and other forms of disparate treatment continued to block opportunities for approximately half of all black and Hispanic home seekers nationwide, whether they were potential home buyers or renters. Fair housing groups have continued to document the same practices through the 1990s.

The Federal Government Reinforces Dual Housing Markets

By concentrating public housing in central city locations and financing highways to facilitate suburban development, the federal government has further reinforced emerging dual housing markets. And by subsidizing the costs of sewer systems, school construction, roads, and other aspects of suburban infrastructure, government policy nurtures urban sprawl, which generally benefits predominantly white outlying communities at the expense of increasingly nonwhite urban and inner-ring suburban communities.

The problem today is not that loan officers or insurance agents are racist. Rather, it's that their decisions are largely dictated by considerations of financial risk—and the evaluation of that risk has often been colored by questions of race. Unfortunately, it is sometimes hard to disentangle discrimination based explicitly on race from discrimination based on the credit and overall financial status of home owners, the condition of the homes they want to purchase, and the state of the neighborhood as it affects property values. Even if race per se is not a leading factor in lending or insurance decisions, urban blacks are more likely to have poor credit ratings and are more likely to be purchasing homes in neighborhoods with lower property values. These factors hurt their mortgage and insurance applications.

The Mortgage Gap

While the federal government actively encouraged racial segregation in the nation's housing markets until the 1960s, since then its official record on prohibiting discrimination has been more favorable. For example, the federal Fair Housing Act of 1968 and the Equal Credit Opportunity Act of 1974 outlawed racial discrimination in mortgage lending and related credit transactions, and in 1975, Congress enacted the Home Mortgage Disclosure Act (HMDA), which requires most mortgage lenders to disclose the geographic location of their mortgage lending activity. In 1989, Congress expanded HMDA to require lenders to report the race, gender, and income of every loan applicant, the census tract location of his or her home, and whether the application was accepted or denied. And in 1977, Congress enacted the Community Reinvestment Act (CRA), requiring depository institutions (primarily commercial banks and savings institutions) to seek out and be responsive to the credit needs of their entire service areas, including low- and moderate-income neighborhoods.

Still, recent research using HMDA data has found that black mortgage loan applicants are denied twice as often as whites. The most comprehensive study, prepared by researchers with the Federal Reserve Bank of Boston and published in the American Economic Review in 1996, found that even among equally qualified borrowers, blacks were rejected 60 percent more often than whites. The causes of this disparity, and particularly the extent to which outright discrimination accounts for them, continue to be hotly debated.

Discrimination Persists

Other research suggests that discrimination of some sort must be stubbornly persisting. Paired testing—an investigative procedure whereby pairs of equally qualified white and nonwhite borrowers or borrowers from white and nonwhite neighborhoods approach the same lenders to inquire about a loan—has found that applicants from black and Hispanic communities are often offered inferior products, charged higher fees, provided less counseling or assistance, or are otherwise treated less favorably than applicants from white communities. Underwriting guidelines like minimum loan amounts and maximum housing age requirements that are used by many lenders also are found to have an adverse disparate impact on minority communities. Over the past seven years the U.S. Department of Justice (DOJ) and the U.S. Department of Housing and Urban Development (HUD) have documented similar practices in settling fair housing complaints with 17 lenders involving millions of dollars in damages to victims and billions of dollars in loan commitments and other services previously denied to minority communities.

Fortunately, there is some evidence that racial gaps are closing. Between 1993 and 1997 the number of home purchase mortgage loans to blacks and Hispanics nationwide increased 60 percent, compared to 16 percent for whites. The percentage of those loans going to black and Hispanic borrowers, therefore, grew from 5 percent to 7 percent for each group. These positive trends likely reflect several developments.

Housing Discrimination Perpetuates Poverty

It is a bitter irony that for much of the 20th century this country's system of property rights was used to deny black Americans their property rights. Levittown, on Long Island, was the first major planned suburb in America, developed in 1947 to help house the GIs returning from World War II and their families. That is, except for the 1.2 million black Americans who served in the war, because each Levittown home came with a restrictive covenant that said, "The tenant agrees not to permit the premises to be used or occupied by any person other than members of the Caucasian race." Even in Washington, D.C., African Americans had trouble closing the purchase of a home because some of the deeds included language that said, "It is covenanted and agreed that the above described property and no part thereof, shall ever be sold, transferred, leased, rented to, nor occupied by any Negro or person of African blood." Such racial covenants were even written into the Federal Housing Administration underwriting manual and weren't outlawed by the Supreme Court until 1948.

Franklin D. Raines, *Sojourners*, September/October 2002.

The multimillion-dollar DOJ and HUD settlements of fair housing complaints certainly attracted the industry's attention. And under the Community Reinvestment Act, community-based advocacy groups have negotiated reinvestment agreements with lenders in approximately 100 cities in 33 states, totaling more than $400 billion in lending commitments. These settlements and agreements call for a variety of actions, including opening new branch offices in central city neighborhoods, advertising in electronic and print media directed at minority communities, hiring more minority loan officers, educating consumers on mortgage lending and home ownership, and developing new loan products. Sources ranging from the National Community Reinvestment Coalition to Federal Reserve Chairman Alan Greenspan maintain that lenders have discovered profitable markets that had previously been underserved due to racial discrimination.

Financial Consolidation Could Encourage Discrimination

Yet this progress may be threatened by consolidation within and across financial industries as well as between financial and commercial businesses. For several years Congress has debated financial modernization legislation that would permit and encourage consolidation activities among banks, insurers, and securities firms that are currently prohibited by various post–Depression era statutes, most notably the Glass-Steagall Act. Even in the absence of such legislation, financial institutions have found loopholes in the laws, and consolidation has occurred within and among financial service industries.

Several studies indicate that mergers and acquisitions decrease CRA performance. The Woodstock Institute, a Chicago-based research and advocacy group that focuses on community reinvestment issues, recently found that small lenders make a higher share of their loans in low-income neighborhoods than do larger lenders. According to John Taylor, president of the National Community Reinvestment Coalition, small, local lenders have an intimate knowledge of their customers that larger and more distant institutions cannot develop. In addition, consolidation across financial industries can result in the shifting of assets away from depositories currently covered by CRA to independent mortgage banks and other institutions not covered by this law.

No Insurance, No Loan

Before potential home owners can apply for a mortgage loan, they must produce proof of insurance. As the Seventh Circuit Court of Appeals stated in its decision in the 1992 case of NAACP v. American Family Mutual Insurance Co., "No insurance, no loan; no loan, no house." Unfortunately, not much is known about the behavior of the property insurance industry, in part because there is no law comparable to HMDA requiring public disclosure of the disposition of applications and geographic location of insured properties. What evidence does exist, however, demonstrates the persistence of substantial racial disparities—though as with mortgage lending businesses, it is impossible to determine precisely to what extent this disparity is due to outright racial discrimination.

In 1992, 33 urban communities voluntarily provided zip code data to their state insurance commissioners on policies written, premiums charged, losses experienced, and other factors. Analysis of the data by the National Association of Insurance Commissioners revealed that even after loss costs were taken into consideration, racial composition of zip codes was strongly associated with the price and number of policies written by these companies. Insurers were underwriting relatively fewer policies for black neighborhood applicants, and the policies they did write were often at higher premiums than for comparable white applicants from white areas.

More recently the National Fair Housing Alliance conducted paired testing of large insurers in nine cities and found evidence of discrimination against blacks and Hispanics in approximately half of the tests. Applicants from minority communities were refused insurance, offered inferior policies, or forced to pay higher premiums. Some applicants from these areas were required to produce proof of inspection or credit reports not required in other areas. Applicants from minority communities were also found to be held to more stringent maximum age and minimum value policy requirements. (Companies sometimes require that a house not be older than a certain age, or have a minimum appraisal value, before they will insure it.)

Racial Gaps Are Closing

But there is evidence here, too, that these racial gaps may be closing, at least in certain markets. Four major insurers (Allstate, State Farm, Nationwide, and American Family), accounting for almost half of all home owners' insurance policies sold nationwide, have settled fair housing complaints since 1995 with HUD, the DOJ, and several fair housing and civil rights organizations. In October 1998 a Richmond jury found Nationwide guilty of intentional discrimination and ordered the insurer to pay more than $100 million in punitive damages to the local fair housing group, Housing Opportunities Made Equal (HOME), which filed the lawsuit. These insurers have agreed to eliminate discriminatory underwriting guidelines, open new offices in minority areas, and market products through minority media to increase service in previously underserved minority communities. At the same time, several insurers, trade associations, and state regulators have launched voluntary initiatives to educate consumers, recruit minority agents and more agents for urban communities, and generally increase business in urban neighborhoods.

As a first step toward greater understanding of the issue, insurance companies should be required to publicly disclose information about the geographic distribution of insurance policies, which would lead to a range of studies just as HMDA did in the mortgage lending field. In addition, researchers should undertake follow-up studies to document the impact of recent legal settlements and indicate what has worked and why. Currently, evaluations of these efforts are included as part of the settlements, but the results are not for public consumption.

Institutions, Not Individuals

Discriminatory practices in the housing industry are often treated as the problem of selected individuals—consumers who happen to have the wrong credit or color, or providers who have prejudicial attitudes and act in discriminatory ways. Thinking this way, one loses sight of the structural and political roots of the problem and of potential solutions. Dismantling our cities' dual housing markets will require appropriate political strategies that address the structural causes.

Several steps should be taken to augment ongoing community reinvestment efforts. First, Congress should enact an insurance disclosure law, comparable to HMDA, that would permit regulators, consumers, and the insurance industry itself to understand better where insurance availability problems persist and why. This information would likely stimulate additional organizing, enforcement, and voluntary industry efforts to respond to remaining problems.

Second, additional paired testing would reveal specific policies and practices (related to pricing, types of products offered, and qualifying standards) that are delivered in a discriminatory manner, enabling enforcement agencies to target their resources and secure more comprehensive remedies.

Congress Must Set Requirements

Third, Congress should establish the following requirements for any significant merger, consolidation, or acquisition involving banks, insurers, securities firms, and related financial industries:

- CRA provisions should assure that all institutions determine and respond to the needs of low-income residents and communities;
- low-cost checking, savings, and other basic banking services should be available to low-income residents;
- regulatory reviews should be conducted of all proposed restructurings to assure that an adequate plan is in place to meet community reinvestment objectives;
- public hearings should be offered on any proposed significant restructuring to permit comment by all parties that would be affected prior to any decision by a regulatory agency on the proposal;
- any subsidiary currently or subsequently found to be in violation of the Fair Housing Act or related fair lending rules should be excluded or divested.

None of these provisions would prohibit lenders, insurers, or other providers of financial services from engaging in transactions they find beneficial. But these guidelines would assure that the products and services of these industries are available throughout all of the nation's metropolitan areas.

Segregation and Poverty Must Be Addressed

If we are to address seriously the segregation and poverty that persist in urban America, we must continue to educate consumers about effective money management and providers of financial services about lingering discrimination. Public officials must also intensify redevelopment efforts in inner cities—once a city can demonstrate tighter labor markets, higher wages, and more jobs, lenders and insurers will start to market their products more aggressively in distressed but recovering areas. But as long as racial discrimination—whether by intent or effect—persists in the housing services industry, our cities will remain divided by segregation, leaving blacks and other minorities in underserved, undesirable locations.

"There is no evidence of significant discrimination in bank lending against prospective minority homebuyers."

Housing Discrimination Has Been Exaggerated

John Hood

In the following viewpoint, John Hood argues that the profit motive inherent in capitalism successfully discourages intentional housing discrimination. He asserts that there is little evidence of discrimination in bank lending for home loans. Hood maintains that in the American capitalist system, mortgage lenders cannot afford to discriminate against applicants based on race or gender. Lenders are concerned only with credit worthiness—the ability to make loan payments on time. He contends, therefore, that housing discrimination does not limit the economic opportunities of minorities. John Hood is president of the John Locke Foundation, a nonprofit think tank.

As you read, consider the following questions:

1. According to Hood, to what triumph are the economic accomplishments and improved prospects for women and minorities almost totally due?
2. What is the key to antidiscrimination, in the author's opinion?
3. To what does Hood ascribe rejection of minority loan applicants?

D o racial minorities, women, and other groups need the government to protect them against prejudice and discrimination? To hear some prominent social commentators tell it, American business has a shameful record on social equality. Corporate boards lack significant minority representation. Minority consumers are underserved, and minority and female workers are underpaid. Minorities and women can't get financing to start their own businesses. "In most fields, there is a level beyond which people of color cannot rise," said Stephen Carter, the well-known author and law professor. Similar complaints about the economic prospects of women have been popularized in recent years by such authors as Susan Faludi and Gloria Steinem.

This picture of the private sector as an arena of continued discrimination, inequality, and despair for everyone in society except white men is often repeated, presumed accurate by reporters and politicians, used to defend government affirmative action programs—and completely wrong. Not only is there great news to report for the economic accomplishments and prospects of previously downtrodden groups in America, but this good news is due almost totally to the triumph of commercial values over alternative values that have in the past put fear, racism, and insularity ahead of business success and profit.

Recent Economic Successes Belie Discrimination

The cornucopia of good news about social equality and American business overflows with little-noticed facts about our recent economic past. For example:

• American women were forming small businesses at twice the rate of men in the early 1990s. Businesses owned by women now employ more people than do all the firms in the Fortune 500 combined. If the trends of the 1980s and early 1990s continue, women will own half of all U.S. businesses by the year 2000. Similarly, the number of businesses owned by members of racial and ethnic minorities more than doubled from 1982 to 1994.

• Before the Second World War, only 5 percent of American blacks had middle-class incomes. Today, the figure is about 60 percent. From 1981 to 1991, the total income of blacks grew 38 percent, faster than the growth rate for the incomes of the white population. Almost half of all black households own their own homes.

• Measured correctly, there is no evidence of significant discrimination in bank lending against prospective minority homebuyers.

• Among full-time, college-educated workers, about the same percentage of blacks and whites have executive, administrative, or managerial jobs.

Competition Is the Key to Ending Discrimination

Naturally, racial stereotypes, invidious discrimination, and animus still exist in America. But it is important to understand the role profit-seeking businesses play in combating these lingering problems. For corporate managers, excluding potential workers or customers because of race, gender, or other group characteristics means sacrificing future productivity and sales. It simply stands to reason that the wider you cast your net for employees or consumers, the better off you will be. To do anything less is to fail in your responsibility to the owners or shareholders.

Gary Becker, Nobel laureate in economics and a professor at the University of Chicago, pointed out the anti-discrimination effect of free enterprise in 1957, and has been restating his conclusion ever since. The key, he says, is competition. Screening out job applicants because of their group means reducing the chances of hiring the best worker, who may well go to work for a competing firm. Similarly, screening out whole groups of consumers means giving up sales to competitors. "Competition forces people to face costs, and therefore reduce the amount of discrimination when compared with monopolistic situations," Becker said. So racism and discrimination are, over time, much more likely to persist in monopolistic institutions (like governments themselves) rather than in businesses. . . .

Race, Gender, and Entrepreneurship

As mentioned, the number of businesses owned by racial minorities and women has been increasing rapidly in recent decades. Not only has the number of firms grown, but their share in the national economy has, too. Just from 1991 to 1995, for example, the combined revenue of the *Black Enterprise* 100 for industrial/service companies and auto dealers grew by 63 percent to $11.7 billion. A third of the roughly 6.5 million enterprises with fewer than 500 employees were owned or controlled by women in 1994. . . .

The Price of Prejudice

Not many businessmen prefer prejudice to profits. As economist Milton Friedman puts it, "A businessman or an entrepreneur who expresses preferences in his business activities that are not related to productive efficiency is at a disadvantage compared to other individuals who do not. Such an individual is in effect imposing higher costs on himself than are other individuals who do not have such preferences. Hence, in a free market, they will tend to drive him out."

George C. Leef, *The Freeman*, February 1981.

In 1994, *Black Enterprise* named [black businessman] A.B. Gaston, then 102 years old, as the magazine's Entrepreneur of the Century. In Gaston's view, his business success has enabled him to advance the cause of racial equality just as his hero Booker T. Washington had predicted. "Money has no color," Gaston said. "If you can build a better mousetrap, it won't matter whether you're black or white, people will buy it."

Color-Blind Customers and Employers

The entrepreneurial explosion among women and members of minorities in the past few years has demonstrated that consumers, both households and businesses, will generally buy from anyone who can supply a high-quality product or service at a low price. The same might be said about American employers, who have discovered that businesses that want to compete effectively cannot afford to discriminate against workers because of race, sex, or other such characteristics. Indeed, having a workforce of people who meet high standards of quality and performance and bring differing backgrounds and perspectives to their jobs is often a recipe for success.

Vigorous political debates about such subjects as affirmative action and comparable worth obscure what is actually occurring in the American economy today: the gradual elimination of discriminatory hiring and firing practices, as well as rising levels of compensation and respect for minority and female workers. According to economist Howard R. Bloch of George Mason University, 70 to 85 percent of observed differences in income and employment among American racial and ethnic groups disappear when you adjust the numbers for factors such as age, education, and experience. "That's been shown by studies dating back to the mid-1960s," Bloch said. "And you can't even be sure that the residual gap is due to discrimination. It could be due to factors we haven't controlled for."

In measurements of accumulated household wealth, as contrasted with annual income, minorities have also made tremendous gains. A Federal Reserve Bank of St. Louis study in 1989 found that observed differences between whites and minorities were no longer statistically significant once age and education were taken into account. "Members of minority groups are typically younger than whites, and therefore have had less time to accumulate assets," noted the author, John C. Weicher of the Hudson Institute. . . .

The Redlining Controversy

The efforts of corporations to cultivate regular customers among minority groups has been largely obscured in the public mind by the lingering controversy over "redlining" by banks, insurers, real estate agents, and similar types of businesses. Discussion of redlining is complicated by the fact that historically, some lenders and insurers were clearly willing to forgo the business of blacks and others to reinforce a social consensus of segregation in their communities. But this despicable—and economically unwise—practice would seem to be extremely rare today, despite incessant claims by activists and the media that redlining remains the rule.

The problem is that studies purporting to show discrimination in bank lending or insurance focus almost exclusively on rejection rates for loans and policies. These rejection rates often do, indeed, differ significantly among racial groups in studies. But these studies ignore many important factors that provide a more plausible explanation for the apparent disparity than does racism. Sometimes the studies promoted so widely by the mass media, like the celebrated 1992 Federal Reserve Board of Boston study purporting to show higher black rejection rates than those of whites with similar incomes, are simply invalid; that study contained transcription and mathematical errors, inappropriate generalizations, and the skewing of average results by a few exceptional cases.

Ironically, higher rejection rates are often found for those very institutions, including minority-owned banks, that are trying to extend credit in inner-city and minority neighborhoods, since banks in predominantly white areas are more likely to receive applicants from a smaller, more select group of minorities with better-than-average financial resources, work histories, or business prospects. When a bank opens a branch in a minority community, it will necessarily reject more minority applications than before.

It is the personal characteristics of loan applicants—the items in their financial history likely to communicate to potential lenders the likelihood that their loans will be repaid—that explain virtually all racial or ethnic disparities. The most important measure of discrimination is not rejection rates, which are affected by a host of racially neutral factors, but instead the rates at which customers of different races or communities default on their loans. If households or businesses in black areas tend to default at lower rates than those in white areas, that would be evidence of discrimination, since blacks would seem to have to meet higher credit standards than whites do to get loans. On the other hand, if the default rates of blacks are higher, that would suggest discrimination in favor of them. In reality, the available evidence on default rates suggests that there is no significant difference between households and businesses of predominantly white and predominantly minority communities, suggesting that the latter are not being "redlined." Other studies that have tried to identify actual racial discrimination by interviewing loan applicants have often failed to find any significant evidence of it.

It is important to understand the role of profit-seeking

business in eliminating disparities in income and economic opportunity that are based on racism and sexism. For groups kept from realizing the American dream by the prejudices and failures of the past, the best hope for progress in the future is an economy populated with companies whose managers put performance and profitability first.

Periodical Bibliography

The following articles have been selected to supplement the diverse views presented in this chapter.

William N. Brownsberger	"Prevalence of Frequent Cocaine Use in Urban Poverty Areas," *Contemporary Drug Problems*, Summer 1997.
Dahleen Glanton	"High Rate of Out-Of-Wedlock Births Keeps Mississippi Mired in Poverty," *Knight Ridder/Tribune News Service*, March 25, 2001.
Ariel Halpern	"Poverty Among Children Born Outside of Marriage: Preliminary Findings from the National Survey of America's Families," Urban Institute, December 1999.
Brian B. Issleb	"Life Ain't Fair: Deal with It," *Daily Illini Online*, July 3, 2001.
Judith Miller Jones, Judith D. Moore, and Michael Black	"Welfare Reform and Substance Abuse: Innovative State Strategies," National Health Policy Forum Issue Brief, March 7, 2002.
Sal F. Marino	"The Devil Is in Discrimination," *Industry Week*, June 21, 1999.
Charles E. Mueller	"Why Is Black America So Poor? Racism and the Punditry Problem," *Antitrust Law and Economics Review*, Spring 2000.
New Statesman	"Wage War on Poverty, Not Drugs," April 3, 2000.
Franklin D. Raines	"40 Acres and a Mortgage: Why Home Ownership Is Key to Achieving Racial Equality," *Sojourners*, September/October 2002.
Jacquelin W. Scarbrough	"Welfare Mothers' Reflections on Personal Responsibility," *Journal of Social Issues*, Summer 2001.
Michael B. Teitz and Karen Chapple	"The Cause of Inner-City Poverty: Eight Hypotheses in Search of Reality," *Cityscape: A Journal of Policy Development and Research*, 1998.
Elizabeth Terry-Humen, Jennifer Manlove, and Kristin A. Moore	"Births Outside of Marriage: Perceptions vs. Reality," Child Trends Research Brief, April 2001.
Richard Weissbourd	"Moral Parent, Moral Child: Family Structure Matters Less to a Child's Development than the Quality of the Parenting," *American Prospect*, July 15, 2002.

Patricia J. Williams | "Of Race and Risk," *Nation*, December 29, 1997.

Work and Family Newsbrief | "Study Says Bias Is Alive and Well," September 2002.

Nicholas Zill | "Hearing on Reducing Nonmarital Births," Testimony Before the Subcommittee on Human Resources of the House Committee on Ways and Means, June 29, 1999. http://waysandmeans.house.gov.

CHAPTER 3

How Can Poor People in the United States Be Helped?

Chapter Preface

Education can provide the surest escape for those born into poverty. No concept is considered more American than the right of people to determine their own destinies through education and hard work, regardless of the circumstances of their birth. Mandatory public education from kindergarten to age eighteen was meant to give every citizen a fair chance—an equal opportunity—to achieve success. However, in the late 1950s and early 1960s, psychologists and education experts determined that children from poor families often lacked the emotional, social, and psychological skills they needed to be kindergarten-ready and able to learn. Moreover, poor children often did not receive adequate nutrition or medical and dental care and were therefore at a physical as well as academic disadvantage from their earliest school days. In 1965 the federal government conceived a program to help meet the needs of disadvantaged preschoolers and give them a head start on the education they would need to lift themselves out of poverty.

Project Head Start, a cornerstone of then-President Lyndon B. Johnson's War on Poverty, was originally an eight-week summer program administered by the Office of Economic Opportunity. It provided comprehensive developmental services for low-income preschoolers and social services for their families. A philosophy new to the federal government—that low-income people should help plan and run their own programs—became critical to the functioning and success of Project Head Start. Parents were involved along with their children in programs that offered not only academic enrichment but also nutritious lunches and snacks and basic health care, including inoculations. Poor parents across the nation wanted to know how to help their children become successful in school, and Head Start programs showed them. In 1969, the Head Start program was moved from the Office of Economic Opportunity to the Office of Child Development in the U.S. Department of Health and Human Services. Now it is a program within the Administration for Children and Families in the U.S. Department of Health and Human Services. Today, Head Start is a full-time program that serves Native American, migrant farmworker, urban and rural children and their families in every state, the District of Columbia, Puerto Rico, the Virgin Islands, and Pacific Insular Areas.

Many studies have been conducted to verify the effectiveness of Project Head Start. All of the studies agree that there are definitive short-term gains; Head Start preschoolers do better in kindergarten and early elementary (first through third) grades than low-income preschoolers who did not attend the program. They are less likely to repeat a grade or be placed in a special education class. However, gains for Head Start participants begin to fade out by third grade if the remainder of their elementary education is of poor quality, as is often the case for low-income youngsters. In elementary and middle schools where follow-up programs for Head Start preschoolers are available, "fade out" decreases significantly, delinquency is diminished, and students are much more likely to graduate from high school.

Critics of the present Head Start program insist that while its original, laudable goal was to prepare poor children for school and enhance their educational opportunities, the program has now become little more than a nurturing day care center with hot meals, medical attention, and social services. They argue that Head Start has no standard curriculum to prepare children for school and ensure cognitive development. Rather, the program's mission is to support "emerging literacy and numeracy development through materials and activities according to the developmental level of each child." These experts suggest that the federal government should revamp Head Start, redesigning the educational component while retaining the nutritional, medical, and social services aspects. In addition, they assert, a well-qualified, better-paid staff should be recruited rather than relying on help from underqualified parents. Many educators maintain that if Head Start were reorganized, it would better serve poor children and their families.

Project Head Start is just one of the programs designed by the government to help low-income families. Authors in the following chapter explore other government programs as well as privately funded efforts to help poor people in America.

"Government benefit programs lifted 27 million . . . people out of poverty, cutting poverty nearly in half."

Government Programs Help the Poor

Wendell Primus and Kathryn Porter

Government programs cut poverty nearly in half in the mid-1990s, Wendell Primus and Kathryn Porter argue in the following viewpoint, which is based on a study they coauthored for the Center on Budget and Policy Priorities (CBPP). Further, government programs reduced the depth of poverty—the degree by which incomes fall below the poverty line—by two-thirds. The authors maintain that the elderly (due to Social Security) and children (due to the Earned Income Tax Credit) benefit most from federal programs. The CBPP is a research and policy institute that analyzes government policies and programs, especially those that apply to low-income people. Wendell Primus is the director of the income security division of the CBPP; Kathryn Porter is a senior research analyst.

As you read, consider the following questions:
1. According to the authors, what was the key reason the poverty rate did not drop in 1996 in spite of economic growth?
2. Which government program has the largest effect on working families, in the authors' opinion?
3. What do the authors maintain happens to the role of the safety net in reducing poverty when the economy slows down?

A new analysis of Census data finds that Social Security reduces the proportion of elderly living in poverty from 50 percent to about 12 percent and lifts 12 million elderly people out of poverty, while the Earned Income Tax Credit—a tax credit for low-income working families—now lifts more children out of poverty than any other government program.

Strengths of the Safety Net, by the Center on Budget and Policy Priorities, also finds the impact of government benefit programs in reducing poverty weakened modestly in 1996, especially among children. The study identifies this as a key reason the poverty rate failed to drop in 1996 despite economic growth.

Even so, the report found, government benefit programs have a large effect in reducing poverty. The incomes that families received through the private economy left 57.5 million people below the poverty line in 1996, the study reported. Government benefit programs lifted 27 million of these 57.5 million people out of poverty, cutting poverty nearly in half.

"An array of programs, led by Social Security, are having strong effects in reducing poverty," said Wendell Primus, the Center's director of income security and co-author of the study. "Without Social Security, poverty among the elderly would be widespread."

Primus noted that in the absence of Social Security and other government benefits, one of every two elderly people would have fallen below the poverty line in 1996. Primarily because of Social Security, fewer than one in 10 elderly Americans was poor that year.

Primus added that an examination of these data over time also shows that when government benefit programs have been strengthened, they have lifted larger proportions of people out of poverty, while fewer people have been lifted out when—as in 1996—the programs have weakened.

The Study Counts Noncash Benefits and Taxes

The study uses unpublished Census data to compare the number of people with incomes below the poverty line *before* receipt of government benefits to those left in poverty *after* government benefits are counted. The difference reflects the number of people the safety net programs remove from poverty.

The study follows the recommendations of a 1995 National Academy of Sciences panel in counting certain non-cash benefits such as food stamps and housing assistance as part of income and in reflecting the effects on income of federal income and payroll taxes and the Earned Income Tax Credit (EITC). As a result, the study's measure of poverty after government benefits are counted shows somewhat lower poverty rates than the official Census Bureau poverty measure, which excludes non-cash benefits and the EITC and measures before-tax rather than after-tax income.

Programs Cut Poverty Nearly in Half

In 1996, the study found, 57.5 million people—21.6 percent of the U.S. population—had incomes below the poverty line before receipt of government benefits. After government benefits are taken into account, the number remaining in poverty was reduced to 30.5 million people, or 11.5 percent of the population. The study also found that government benefit programs reduce the *depth* of poverty—the degree to which families' incomes fall below the poverty line before receipt of government benefits—by two-thirds.

The study found that government benefit programs, sometimes referred to as safety net programs, have their most striking effects on the elderly. Some 50.1 percent of the elderly population would have been poor in 1996 in the absence of government benefits, the study reported. Government benefit programs lowered the elderly poverty rate to 9.2 percent.

The strong effect of government benefits in reducing poverty among the elderly is due overwhelmingly to Social Security. In 1996, Social Security was responsible for nine of every ten elderly people lifted out of poverty by government benefit programs. The safety net programs lifted a total 13 million elderly people out of poverty, with Social Security responsible for lifting out 11.7 million of these 13 million people.

Government benefits lift from poverty more than four of every five elderly people who otherwise would be poor, the

study found, but fewer than one in three children who otherwise would be poor. In 1996, government benefit programs lowered the child poverty rate from 23.6 percent before receipt of government benefits to 16.1 percent after receipt of benefits.

The Earned Income Tax Credit, expanded under Presidents [Ronald] Reagan, [George] Bush and [Bill] Clinton, emerged in 1996 as the single program removing the largest number of children from poverty, the study reported. The EITC, which offsets some or all of federal income and payroll taxes and, in many cases, also provides a wage supplement to low-income working families, lifted 4.6 million people—including 2.4 million children—from poverty in 1996.

Elderly Lifted Out of Poverty by Social Security as Percentage of All Elderly Lifted Out of Poverty by Safety Net Programs, 1996

	Number (millions)	As Percentage of All Elderly Who Are Lifted Out of Poverty
Elderly lifted out of poverty by:		
Social Security	11.7	89.3%
Other social insurance	0.4	3.1%
Means-tested cash	0.5	3.7%
Means-tested non-cash	0.5	3.8%
All safety net programs	13.0	100.0%

Center on Budget and Policy Priorities, March 9, 1998.

Although the EITC has the largest effect in lifting children out of poverty, cash assistance and food and housing programs have a larger impact than the EITC in diminishing the severity of poverty among children. Many of the children whose families receive cash assistance are so poor that this aid renders them less poor rather than lifting them above the poverty line.

Since the EITC is available only to working families, its effects on children in those families are especially strong, the study found. Among working families, the EITC has a larger effect than any other program or category of programs both in reducing the number of poor children and in reducing the severity of poverty among those who remain poor.

The EITC's effects are largest in the South, the region in which wages tend to be lowest and the proportion of working families with poverty-level incomes is highest. Nearly half of all children in the South who were lifted out of poverty by government benefit programs were raised from poverty by the EITC.

Weakening of the Safety Net for Children

The study found that despite the strengthened effects of the EITC in 1996, government benefits lifted out of poverty a smaller percentage of children who would otherwise have been poor than in the previous year. Overall, the benefit programs lifted about 400,000 fewer children from poverty in 1996 than in 1995.

This decline in the impact of the programs, while modest, was sufficient to prevent the child poverty rate, as well as the overall poverty rate, from dropping. Between 1995 and 1996, the poverty rate for children before receipt of government benefits declined modestly, reflecting improvements in the economy. But after receipt of government benefits, the child poverty rate remained essentially unchanged between the two years. The negative effect of a weakening safety net offset the positive effect of a growing economy, the study found.

From 1995 to 1996, the number of children receiving cash public assistance benefits fell 600,000, while the number receiving food stamps fell about 700,000. Improvement in the economy can explain only part of these declines, the study said. It noted that among children who were poor before receipt of government benefits, the proportions receiving public assistance and food stamps fell in 1996.

The welfare law enacted in August 1996 was not a major reason for this decline, according to the study, as few of the legislation's major impacts were felt that year. Many states already had policies in place that were causing caseloads to drop.

The study explained that with these state efforts continuing and the welfare law taking effect, the decline in the number of children receiving food stamps and cash public assistance became sharper in 1997, with the number of children receiving these benefits falling by much larger amounts than can be attributed to continued economic growth. This suggests the proportions of poor children receiving these forms of assistance are likely to have fallen significantly in 1997 and that the safety net's effect in reducing child poverty could be weakening further. Poverty data for 1997 will be available later this year.

The New Trend Could Reverse a Long-Term Pattern

This developing trend of a weakening safety net for families with children could begin to reverse a decade-long pattern. The Center's report compares the effects of government programs on poverty in 1987 and 1996, two similar points in the business cycle. During this period, significant changes in safety net programs occurred. In the years prior to enactment of the welfare law, the EITC expanded, more low-income disabled children became eligible for SSI, and food stamp benefits were improved. As a result, despite the modest weakening of the safety net between 1995 and 1996, government benefit programs still had a greater impact in reducing poverty in 1996 than in 1987.

But if safety net programs reduced poverty more than in 1996 then in 1987, the economy had a smaller impact. The poverty rate as measured before receipt of government benefits—the measure that reflects the impact of the economy by itself—was actually higher in 1996 than in 1987, even though the unemployment rate was significantly lower.

"Despite remarkable progress in reducing unemployment, the economy is performing less well than in previous recoveries in lifting people out of poverty," study co-author Kathryn Porter said. "As a result, the role of the safety net in reducing poverty takes on added significance."

*"Those in need are best served by private
efforts in a free society."*

Government Programs Have
Not Helped the Poor

J.D. Tuccille

Government programs do not do much to help the poor—in
fact, they encourage bad behavior—J.D. Tuccille argues in
the following viewpoint. He contends that the poverty rate is
greater today than in 1965 when the War on Poverty began,
although the government has spent $5 trillion on antipoverty
programs. He contends that most of the money spent on
such programs goes to support the welfare-poverty industry,
not to help poor people. Moreover, he maintains, government programs disrupt social bonds and encourage dependency. J.D. Tuccille is the editor of *Free-Market.Net Spotlight*.

As you read, consider the following questions:
1. According to the NCPA study, what is one reason the
   War on Poverty is not being won?
2. In the author's opinion, what caused the wave of welfare
   reform efforts in the 1990s?
3. What does Leslie Siddeley claim contributed to the
   decline of private charity?

E very advocate of tamed government faces an inevitable challenge: "Don't you care about the poor?"

The unstated assumption in the question, of course, is that among the many responsibilities of government is the task of feeding, clothing, and bootstrapping those who are unable to care for themselves. In our skepticism about the role of government, we libertarians are apparently giddy with delight at the thought of prancing over the prone forms of the homeless hordes that are destined to wash up on the shores of a free society.

But for such a callous bunch, we seem to spend a lot of time considering the plight of those who are down on their luck. The criticism targeted at the welfare state by small-government advocates is rarely of the Dickensian "let them starve" variety. Instead, critics maintain that government social services provide little in the way of help, and lots in the way of incentives for bad behavior.

Writing in 1994 for the National Center for Policy Analysis (NCPA), [NCPA is a public policy organization whose goal is to develop private alternatives to government control] John C. Goodman, Gerald W. Reed, and Peter S. Ferrara pointed out that, "[s]ince 1965 we have spent $5 trillion on the War on Poverty, measured in 1992 constant dollars. Yet the poverty rate is higher today than it was the year the War on Poverty began."

According to this NCPA study, one reason the War on Poverty isn't being won is that "most of the money we spend doesn't go to poor people. It goes to nonpoor people who work in the welfare-poverty industry."

An even larger problem with the welfare state, says the Cato Institute's Michael Tanner, is that it disrupts social bonds. He told the U.S. Senate in 1995 that, "welfare contributes to the rise in out-of-wedlock births and single-parent families." This was the point made by Charles Murray in his now-classic 1984 book *Losing Ground*.

The Welfare State Has Failed

Because of the obvious failings of the welfare state, there was a wave of reform efforts in the 1990's.

Some of the reforms have borne fruit. The Heritage Foundation's Robert Rector and Sarah Youssef "found that differences in state welfare policies, specifically stringency of sanctions and timing of work requirements, were highly successful in explaining rapid rates of caseload decline."

But to many critics, welfare reform adds up to minor redecoration. It leaves bureaucrats with an awesome amount of power and responsibility, and the rest of us with little choice in the matter. The better choice, say many, is letting people help each other (*gasp*) voluntarily.

Government Programs Do Not Work

It is time to quit pretending that government programs are "helping," and acknowledge that they are failures and perhaps people are better off genuinely volunteering to help others. History proves that common people who genuinely volunteer with their time, heart and substance will have a much better opportunity to influence for good than an overworked government bureaucracy.

Rachel Alexander, *Arizona Daily Wildcat*, March 8, 1999.

When people's personal preferences are allowed to guide their charitable instincts, they can prod social service organizations into abandoning bad policies in favor of approaches that might work.

The recent case of the Broadway Presbyterian Church in New York City is a good example. When church members noticed that their soup kitchen was becoming *way* too popular, they migrated to a more rigorous work-for-food approach that saw quick results.

Private Charities Are Successful

That private charities can do good should come as no surprise. After all, that's there was before the welfare state, and poverty didn't seem to balloon then in quite so modern a fashion as it does under the management of well-financed bureaucrats. Well into the twentieth century, fraternal groups provided their members with the full range of what are now considered social services (hey, you knew there was a reason Gramps joined the Moose Lodge, right?).

If private efforts were so successful, why have single moms

become political footballs on the legislative gridiron?

In a Humane Studies Review piece on fraternal groups, Leslie Siddeley suggests that the decline of private charity was due to a double-whammy combination of death by red tape and the tax-funded provision of government alternatives. After all, if you're already coughing up taxes for a compulsory serving of goodies, why spend your scarce dollars on the same thing?

Could private groups once again take on the full provision of charity? Could they shoulder what has become a multi-trillion dollar burden?

Private Charities Are Efficient

The Acton Institute's Reverend Robert A. Sirico has written that, "[i]n the post-welfare age, private charity must take on a greater role, but one very different from that which the welfare state traditionally has played. There need not be a dollar-for-dollar replacement of existing expenses: Private charity is much more efficient."

On a slightly different note, the Libertarian Alliance's Brian Micklethwait recommends that helping those in need should be looked at as part of the larger picture of maintaining a free and prosperous society. Says he, "[h]istorically, it is capitalism which has rescued the poor and unfortunate from their plight, insofar as anything ever has, not charity."

Such views may not be completely compatible, but both Sirico and Micklethwait would likely agree that, to answer the inevitable question, they *do* care about the poor, and those in need are best served by private efforts in a free society.

"Today's minimum wage shortchanges
workers and undermines the long-term
health of businesses, communities and the
economy."

Increasing the Minimum Wage Can Help the Working Poor

Holly Sklar

In the following viewpoint, Holly Sklar contends that Americans who earn the minimum wage do not earn a living wage. She argues that a couple with two children would have to work a combined 3.3 full-time minimum-wage jobs to survive. Worker productivity has increased dramatically since 1968, she insists, but the minimum wage has not even kept pace with inflation. Increasing the minimum wage to eight dollars an hour, indexed to inflation, she maintains, would provide a living wage for the average single worker. Holly Sklar is coauthor of *Raise the Floor: Wages and Policies That Work for Us All.*

As you read, consider the following questions:

1. When was the federal minimum wage enacted, as reported by the author?
2. According to Sklar, if wages had kept pace with increasing productivity, what would the minimum have been in 2000?
3. What three benefits do employers realize when employees are paid a living wage, in the author's opinion?

A job should keep you out of poverty, not keep you in it. Most Americans believe that. But as we celebrate Labor Day, hardworking Americans paid minimum wage earn just $10,712 a year. That's a third less than their counterparts earned a third of a century ago—adjusting for inflation.

A couple with two children would have to work a combined 3.3 full-time minimum wage jobs to make ends meet. That's 132 hours a week. It just doesn't add up.

We're in the year 2001 in the richest nation on earth and yet millions of Americans make wages so low they have to choose between eating or heating, health care or child care.

They are health care aides who can't afford health insurance. They work in the food industry, but depend on food banks to help feed their children.

They are child care teachers who don't make enough to save for their own children's education. They care for the elderly, but they have no pensions.

Today's minimum wage and other public policies are not working for many working Americans. Families need more than double the official poverty level to make ends meet.

No State Should Be Allowed to "Opt Out"

The federal minimum wage, first enacted in 1938, was meant to put a firm floor under workers and their families, strengthen the depressed economy by increasing consumer purchasing power, create new jobs to meet rising demand and stop a "race to the bottom" of employers moving to cheaper labor states. President [George W.] Bush's proposal to let states "opt out" of the federal minimum wage would destroy it, taking us back to the pre–New Deal era.

In recent decades, the minimum wage floor has fallen, dragging down average real wages as well. The real value of the minimum wage peaked in 1968 at $7.92 per hour (in 2000 dollars). Since then, worker productivity went up, but wages went down. Productivity grew 74.2 percent between 1968 and 2000, but hourly wages for average workers fell 3 percent, adjusting for inflation. Real wages for minimum wage workers—two-thirds of whom are adults—fell 35 percent.

If wages had kept pace with rising productivity since 1968, the average hourly wage would have been $24.56 in 2000, rather than $13.74. The minimum wage would be $13.80—not $5.15.

Profits also went up, but wages went down. Domestic corporate profits rose 64 percent since 1968, adjusting for inflation. The retail trade industry employs more than half the nation's hourly employees paid at or below minimum wage. Retail profits jumped even higher than profits generally, skyrocketing 158 percent since 1968. The minimum wage would be $13.02 if had kept pace with domestic profits and $20.46 if it had risen with retail profits.

Federal Minimum Wage Should Be Increased to Eight Dollars

CEO pay went up, but workers' wagas went down. In 1980, the average CEO at a major corporation made as much as 97 minimum wage workers. In 2000, they made as much as 1,223 minimum wage workers.

The federal minimum wage can and should be increased to $8 per hour and indexed to inflation. That's the average amount needed for a single full-time worker to meet basic needs such as food, housing, utilities and health care. It matches the 1968 minimum wage peak, adjusting for inflation. To assure that all working families can meet their basic needs we should supplement a higher minimum wage with improved child care, health care and Earned Income Tax Credit policies, for example.

Minimum Wage Statistics

- 71 percent of the workers who benefited from the 1996–97 [minimum wage] increase were adults over 20 years of age.

- Overall, 58 percent of the workers who benefited from the last increase were women.

- Almost half (46 percent) of the workers who benefited from the last increase work full time and an additional 33 percent work between 20 and 34 hours per week.

- 40 percent of minimum wage workers are the sole breadwinners in their family.

- Among teens earning the minimum wage, more than half were in families with below-average incomes.

Ed Mayne, *Utah Business*, January 2002.

Certainly, employers can pay a minimum wage equivalent to what their counterparts paid more than three decades ago. After the last minimum wage increases in 1996–97, the economy boomed with extraordinarily high growth, low inflation, low unemployment and declining poverty rates—until the Federal Reserve purposefully slowed economic growth by raising interest rates, a mistaken course it has since reversed.

Successful businesses—large and small—have shown that good wages are good business. Higher wages reduce turnover, improve productivity and increase purchasing power.

Low Wages Shortchange Workers

In-N-Out Burger, for example, ranks first among fast food chains in food quality, value and customer service. There are more than 150 In-N-Out Burgers in California, Nevada and Arizona. The starting wage of a part-time worker is $8 an hour.

In the words of Philadelphia small business owners Tim Styer, Judy Wicks and Hal Taussig, "All our businesses pay well above the federal minimum wage. We know that today's minimum wage shortchanges workers and undermines the long-term health of businesses, communities and the economy."

Let's stop shortchanging workers with the minimum wage. Let's make it a living.

"Minimum-wage laws increase unemployment among the least skilled, least experienced and minority workers."

Increasing the Minimum Wage Is Counterproductive

Thomas Sowell

In the following viewpoint, Thomas Sowell argues that if the minimum wage is increased, low-skilled people will be excluded from the job market because employers who have to pay higher wages will want more experienced workers with better skills. The least skilled, least experienced, and minority workers will suffer most, he maintains. Further, Sowell claims that most minimum-wage earners are young, entry-level workers who will eventually better themselves through experience and education and therefore do not need artificially raised wages to survive. Thomas Sowell is a senior fellow at the Hoover Institution, a public policy research center at Stanford University, and a nationally syndicated columnist.

As you read, consider the following questions:
1. According to Sowell, more than half of all minimum-wage earners fall into which age bracket?
2. What is the real minimum wage, in the author's opinion?
3. What does Sowell argue is more important to young people than their first paycheck?

Thomas Sowell, "Minimum Wage Misrepresented, Misnamed by Politically Correct," *Insight on the News*, vol. 17, August 20, 2001, p. 46. Copyright © 2001 by *Insight on the News*. Reproduced by permission.

A front-page story about minimum wages in the *Wall Street Journal* illustrates what is wrong with contemporary journalism as much as it illustrates anything about the minimum-wage law. The first nine paragraphs deal with one individual who is wholly atypical of people earning the minimum wage. She is a 46-year-old single mother who works full time.

Way back on page 10, we learn from a small chart that slightly more than one-half of the people earning the minimum wage are from 16 to 24 years of age. Slightly more than one-half of the minimum-wage earners are working part time. Nevertheless, the atypical middle-aged single mother now is brought back into the story again and covered for an additional 13 paragraphs on the inside page.

Three out of four pictures under the heading "The Faces of Low-Wage Work" are of women older than age 40, including one who is 76. This is clever propaganda, but it is lousy journalism. People don't buy a newspaper to be deceived.

Most Minimum Wage Earners Are Young

While the *Wall Street Journal* has one of the most intelligent editorial pages anywhere, some of its news stories on social issues—as distinguished from financial issues—too often are examples of the kind of mushy and even biased journalism that gives political correctness a bad name.

The politically correct party line on minimum wage is that people cannot afford to raise their families on low pay, so the government has to force employers to provide "a living wage" for families. But the vast majority of people making minimum wage are youngsters just beginning their careers. They are not going to flip hamburgers or sweep floors all their lives. Most have better sense than to have children they cannot feed and house.

Yet the main focus of this long article is on a small minority who have a "minimum-wage career." Our atypical middle-aged single mother is invoked once again: "In Ms. Williams' case, practically everyone she knows has been mired in such occupations their whole working lives." Is it supposed to be news that birds of a feather flock together?

Are we supposed to base national policy on one woman's

experience? If we wanted to watch Oprah Winfrey [a popular talk show], would we be reading the *Wall Street Journal?*

The Real Minimum Wage Is Zero

What about those minimum-wage earners who are just passing through that income bracket on their way up: Most of the people in the bottom 20 percent of the income distribution—"the poor"—also are in the top 20 percent at some other point in their lives, when they are counted among "the rich." Usually they are not "poor" the first time nor "rich" the second time, but such is the state of political rhetoric.

The reality of what happens to people over time gets far less attention than one middle-aged single mother working at a minimum-wage job—and, incidentally, receiving government subsidies.

The minimum-wage law very cleverly is misnamed. The real minimum wage is zero. That is what many inexperienced and low-skilled people receive as a result of legislation that makes it illegal to pay them what they are currently worth to an employer.

Most economists long have recognized that minimum-wage laws increase unemployment among the least skilled, least experienced and minority workers. With a little experience, these workers are likely to be worth more.

A Minimum Wage Increase Will Hurt Entry-Level Workers

Many entrepreneurs say living-wage laws end up hurting rather than helping low-income workers by removing them from employers' radar screens. "If I have to start at $12.25 an hour, I will go to hospitality schools to hire," says Paul Hortobagyi, general manager of the 56-employee Georgian Hotel, located in the heart of Santa Monica's tourist zone. "People like my front-desk manager, who started here five years ago as a waiter and couldn't string three sentences together, won't get those chances."

BusinessWeek Online, October 29, 2001.

But they cannot move up the ladder if they can't get on the ladder. That is the real tragedy of the real minimum wage—zero. It is not just the money that these young people miss. It is the experience that can turn out to be far more valuable to them than the first paychecks they take home.

Minimum Wage in America Makes the Third World Suffer

This is especially tragic in the Third World, where multinational corporations may be pressured into setting wages well above what the local labor-market conditions justify. This pressure often comes from self-righteous people back home who mount shrill demonstrations in the mistaken belief that they are helping poor people overseas.

Half a century ago, Professor Peter Bauer of the London School of Economics pointed out that "a striking feature of many underdeveloped counties is that money wages are maintained at high levels" while "large numbers are seeking but unable to find work."

These people can least afford to get the minimum wage of zero just so their would-be saviors can feel noble or so labor unions in Europe and America can price them out of a job to protect their own members' jobs.

"Welfare reform is helping millions of people climb out of poverty."

Welfare Reform Is Effective

U.S. Department of Health and Human Services

In the following viewpoint, the U.S. Department of Health and Human Services (HHS) argues that the welfare reform program begun in 1996 has been successful in combating poverty and helping families work toward self-sufficiency. HHS contends that the welfare caseload has decreased 56 percent nationwide. Moreover, the percentage of American families living below the federal poverty level dropped from 13.7 percent to 11.3 percent, including a significant decrease in the number of children living in poverty. Requiring welfare recipients to work, the department maintains, is key to welfare reform's continued success. HHS oversees all federal welfare and benefit programs.

As you read, consider the following questions:
1. In addition to work, what did President Bush's TANF proposal include?
2. Compared to the original reform program, how many more hours of work does President Bush's proposal require?
3. According to HHS, what is the only way to escape poverty?

U.S. Department of Health and Human Services, "President's TANF Proposal Good for Families: Work, Education, Training Provisions Send Welfare Reform to Next Level," www.hhs.gov, March 5, 2002.

President [George W.] Bush's proposal to reauthorize the Temporary Assistance for Needy Families (TANF) program takes the next step in welfare reform by strengthening work requirements, providing the assistance families need to climb the career ladder and granting states more flexibility to run successful programs [The program was reauthorized.].

"Welfare reform in America worked, despite the dire warnings six years ago by advocacy groups who opposed our efforts to break the cycle of dependency," [U.S. Department of Health and Human Services] Secretary [Tommy] Thompson said. "With President Bush's ambitious and bold proposal, we are taking the next step in welfare reform—one that will help families work toward self-sufficiency.

"Under the old Aid to Families with Dependent Children (AFDC) program, everyone was in poverty. What's worse, they had no way out," Secretary Thompson said. "Welfare reform is helping millions of people climb out of poverty. Now, we want to go the next step and help them climb the job ladder by creating more opportunities for education and job training."

The President's Proposal Increases Flexibility

That's why the centerpiece of President Bush's proposal is work, coupled with new education, training and substance abuse allowances that will help families climb the career ladder and develop the skills necessary to do so.

The President's proposal:

- Requires a 40-hour work week by welfare recipients (up from the current 30 hours). At the same time, however, the President wants to give states more flexibility to count education, job training or substance abuse treatment as work. Therefore, the proposal would require that only 24 hours be spent in the workplace.
- Further, three months out of every 24 months could be used for substance abuse treatment.
- Expands the federal government's waiver authority in major welfare programs (food stamps, housing, workforce programs, adult education) so states will have the flexibility needed to improve the effectiveness and efficiency of these programs.

U.S. Census Bureau Confirms Welfare Reform's Success in 2001

Just consider new data from the U.S. Census Bureau. On Sept. 24 [2002], it released its official poverty count for 2001—a year of tough economic times and increased unemployment, which critics argued would be the real test of welfare reform.

So, did welfare caseloads and child-poverty rates go up? No. Welfare caseloads continued to decrease, and child-poverty rates remained at low levels, including a new record low for African-American children.

These data show that welfare reform is continuing to help hold down poverty rates, despite the recent dips in the economy. It is a tremendously hopeful sign that the groups most likely to collect welfare, and thus be affected by the pro-work reforms in place since 1996, continue to make progress against poverty. Especially given the recent recession, this is further evidence that reform—and not the economy—is the primary reason that work and earnings have increased while caseloads and poverty have been reduced.

Wally Herger, *Insight on the News*, October 15, 2002.

- Maintains the current levels of the TANF block grant at $16.5 billion a year through 2007, giving states the resources they need to build stronger programs and help families achieve self-sufficiency by climbing the career ladder.

The $16.5 billion funding will allow states to assist more families than when the program was originally passed in 1996 due to welfare caseload decreases of 56 percent nationwide.

Work Is the Key

Secretary Thompson called on advocacy groups seeking to make reducing poverty the main priority of welfare reform to endorse the President's proposal, saying "The only way to escape poverty is through work."

Welfare reform has been successful in combating poverty in the United States. Since 1996, when the welfare reform bill was signed into law:

- The percentage of American families with incomes below the federal poverty level dropped from 13.7 percent to 11.3 percent.

- The percentage of children living in poverty fell from 20.5 percent to 16.2 percent.
- The rate of poverty among African-American children in 2000 was the lowest on record, and the poverty rate among Hispanic children had its largest four-year decrease in history between 1996 and 2000.

"Right now, we have the opportunity to build upon the obvious successes of 1996 and take that very important next step," Secretary Thompson said. "There is bipartisan support for this next step because we all know that work builds dignity, self reliance and good habits for life."

6

> *"The welfare reform policy adopted by the [President Bill] Clinton administration and the Republican Congress is devastating millions of US families."*

Welfare Reform Harms the Poor

Debra Watson

When the Temporary Assistance for Needy Families (TANF) program was enacted as part of welfare reform in 1996, it contained some of the most vindictive measures aimed at the poor in the past fifty years, Debra Watson argues in the following viewpoint. She contends that the support provided by the U.S. safety net of social services has reached its lowest level in a generation, with 1.6 million more children living in poverty in 1998 than in 1979. Debra Watson is a writer for the World Socialist Web Site, an information site devoted to the socialist political movement.

As you read, consider the following questions:

1. According to Watson, why did the pace of poverty decline significantly after 1993?
2. What happened to the Food Stamp Program as a result of TANF, in the author's opinion?
3. What benefit for low-income workers does Watson argue is being threatened by accusations of abuse?

Debra Watson, "Poverty and Hunger Worsen Under U.S. Welfare Reform," http://wsws.org, January 12, 2000. Copyright © 2000 by the International Committee of the Fourth International. Reprinted with permission.

Mounting evidence of deepening poverty in the US reveals that the welfare reform policy adopted by the [President Bill] Clinton administration and the Republican Congress is devastating millions of US families. A December 1999 report entitled *Recent Changes in the Impact of the Safety Net on Child Poverty* found sharp increases in extreme poverty on the one hand, and little, if any, improvement in overall conditions for the majority of children in low-income families.

Kathryn Porter and Wendell Primus, the authors of the report, are researchers at the Center on Budget and Policy Priorities (CBPP), a Washington think tank. Their research found that poverty trends, which had been documented using initial post–welfare reform data, continued into 1998. Using previously unpublished statistics on child poverty for 1998, which were compiled by the US Census Bureau, their report concentrates on demonstrating the impact of welfare reform on children. While the Clinton administration continues to insist that "welfare reform is working," many studies have reported increased hunger and homelessness among families with children.

The Personal Responsibility and Work Opportunity Reconciliation Act (PRWORA) was passed by the US Congress and signed by Clinton in 1996. Temporary Assistance for Needy Families (TANF) replaced Aid to Families with Dependent Children, the decades-old safety net for families with children. This act also contained some of the most vindictive measures aimed at the poor since the first federal assistance programs were adopted during the Great Depression of the 1930s. Among other things, it set a five-year lifetime limit for cash assistance and gave the states power to adopt stringent restrictions in several other areas.

Welfare Cuts Mean More Poor Children

The CBPP study found that the welfare cuts had nearly offset any gains from the "longest peacetime economic recovery in US history." Employment and earnings among low-income parents have increased, but benefits have been sharply cut. The result is that while "the number of children living in poverty has declined significantly since 1993," after 1995 the pace of decline dropped dramatically. "Measured on an annual basis, the number of poor children declined at a rate of 1.2 million per year between 1993 and 1995 and at a rate of 400,000 a year—one-third as much—between 1995 and 1998."

Even with the gains due to the reduction in unemployment, the number and percentage of poor children was still higher in 1998 than in 1979. There were 1.6 million more children in poverty in the US in 1998 than in 1979, even after taking into account cash assistance, other social programs and tax credits.

The level of support provided by the US social safety net program has reached the lowest level in a generation, with fewer poor children receiving cash assistance or Food Stamps than in any year since 1970. Cash assistance from TANF has been largely terminated by the 1996 legislation. But even the Food Stamp Program, which was not supposed to be affected by welfare reform, has been cut back sharply. In 1993, some 85 out of 100 poor children received Food Stamps, and this figure rose to 88 out of 100 in 1995. In 1998, by contrast, only 72 out of every 100 poor children received Food Stamps. The Clinton administration has thus presided over cuts in aid to the poor every bit as drastic and heartless as those carried out under the Reagan administration in the 1980s.

Another CBPP study finds large decreases in income among the poorest families particularly since 1995, as the first welfare reform initiatives bore their bitter fruit. These early measures were undertaken by some states under waivers granted by the Clinton administration. Primus produced another report earlier in 1999 showing that from 1995 to 1997 the average disposable income of the poorest 20 percent of single mothers fell by 7.6 percent; the average disposable income of the poorest 10 percent fell by 15.2 percent.

The new CBPP report concentrates on children and updates some of these earlier findings with new US Census Department data. It notes that while the number of children in poverty has declined since 1993, the fall in the aggregate child poverty gap, or the amount of money needed to lift all children out of poverty, has not declined by the same proportion.

Children Fall Deeper into Poverty After Welfare Reform

The CBPP authors highlight the two distinct periods of the Clinton administration: before and after welfare reform. "The reason the child poverty gap changed so little between 1995 and 1998, despite strong economic growth and a decline in the number of poor children, is that the children who remained poor became poorer, on average." In fact, 1998 represents the largest poverty gap per poor child recorded since this data was first collected in 1979.

In 1995, before welfare reform, poor children fell an average of $1,471 below the poverty line. By 1998, they fell an average of $1,604 below the poverty line. Taking into account the unrealistically low official poverty line, this is a considerable amount. In 1998 the US poverty level was $13,133 for a single parent with two children and $16,530 for a couple with two children. A per-child poverty gap of $1,604 translates into a shortfall of $6,416 for a poor family of four persons, leaving an income that is less than two-thirds of the amount that the government considers a bare minimum.

The report notes that based on the 1998 Census figures, "Before counting government benefits and taxes, the per child poverty gap was $2,489, the smallest recorded per child poverty gap before counting government programs. This shows that while the growth of the economy and increases in employment and earnings were working to reduce the depth of poverty among children, the weakening of the safety net was great enough to offset this effect and to increase the depth of poverty among children."

The report also documented the benefits of the Earned Income Tax Credit (EITC) enacted in 1975. Changes made in 1993 to the credit became fully effective in 1996 and further reduced the tax burden for low-income workers, offsetting for some the effects of the cuts in social programs. But allegations in the US Congress of rampant abuse of the EITC are a sign that this benefit for low-income workers is also threatened. The official testimony surrounding the controversy completely ignored evidence that, like the Food Stamp program, the EITC is actually grossly underutilized.

7

"Communities with more households headed by married couples are beset by fewer social ills, such as crime and welfare dependency, than communities where marriage is less prevalent."

Promoting Marriage Will Help End Poverty

Wade F. Horn

In the following viewpoint, Wade F. Horn argues that since marriage provides the most physically, emotionally, and financially stable environment for raising children, the U.S. government should do everything possible to encourage healthy marriages. Further, he maintains, all financial disincentives to marriage, including tax laws and welfare policies, should be changed to favor married over unmarried people. Federal money, he contends, should be spent on marriage-education classes for low-income couples to help them acquire the skills they need to maintain long-term relationships. Wade F. Horn is assistant secretary for children and families in the Department of Health and Human Services.

As you read, consider the following questions:
1. According to Horn, why should low-income couples, particularly, be encouraged to marry?
2. In the author's opinion, how are cohabiting couples different from married couples?
3. What percentage of couples does Horn maintain get married at some point in their lives?

Wade F. Horn, "Q: Should Congress Steer Some Welfare Funds Toward Pro-Marriage Programs? Yes: Healthy Marriages Provide Numerous Benefits to Adults, Children, and Society," *Insight on the News*, vol. 18, March 18, 2002, pp. 40–43. Copyright © 2002 by News World Communications, Inc. Reproduced by permission.

The case for marriage is beyond debate. Marriage is the most stable and healthy environment for raising children. Men and women who are married have been shown to be happier and healthier. And they make more money over time than their single counterparts. Communities with more households headed by married couples are beset by fewer social ills, such as crime and welfare dependency, than communities where marriage is less prevalent.

We really can't argue—or, at least, the data say we shouldn't argue—about the benefits of marriage to children, adults and society. But I do grant that it is reasonable to debate the proper role of government in promoting marriage and that, indeed, reasonable people can disagree on whether government has a place in the marriage debate. I for one, noting that marriage is related directly to child well-being, conclude that government has no choice but to promote healthy marriages.

Let's pose the question this way: Since we know marriage can help adults be happier and healthier, and help children grow up happier and healthier, don't we have a responsibility to figure out ways to help low-income couples who want to be married enjoy a strong, supportive marriage? Of course we do.

Before I lay out my vision for how government can begin to make this happen, allow me a preemptive strike against the criticism that descends every time I unequivocally state that government should support and promote healthy marriages. Let me discuss four things that promoting marriage is not about.

No Matchmaking or Abusive Marriages Allowed

First, it is not about government matchmaking or telling anybody to get married. Obviously, government has no business doing that. Choosing to get married is a private decision. Government should, and will not get into the business of telling people who, or even whether, to marry. I can state without hesitation that the Bush administration has no plans to create a federal dating service. We have no plans to add an entirely new meaning to the famous phrase, "Uncle Sam Wants You!"

Second, promoting marriage cannot, intentionally or inadvertently, result in policies that trap anyone in an abusive relationship. Seeing more Americans married is not our goal. Seeing more Americans enjoying healthy marriages is our goal. Healthy marriages are good for children and adults alike. Abusive marriages are not good for anyone.

Abuse of any sort by a spouse cannot be tolerated under any circumstances, and no marriage-promotion effort should provide comfort to spouse or child abusers. The good news is that good marriages are not a matter of luck but, rather, a matter of skill. We can teach couples the skills necessary to have good marriages. We can teach couples how to negotiate conflict and how not to allow unresolved anger to escalate. Marriages that last a lifetime and marriages that dissolve after a short while often face equal amounts of conflict. The difference is that couples who stay married have learned to manage this conflict constructively. We have proven strategies for teaching these skills to couples; standing by and not sharing these skills with low-income couples is irresponsible.

Third, when we talk about promoting marriage we are not talking about withdrawing support and services for single-parent families. As noted, we are for marriage because that's what the data say is best for kids. There is no data suggesting that taking away support from single mothers helps children in any way. Many single parents make heroic efforts to raise their children despite incredible pressures. Promoting marriage and supporting single parents is not, and must not be, mutually exclusive. Together, they are part of an integrated effort to promote child well-being.

Marriage? Yes! Cohabitation? No!

Finally, marriage promotion is not the same as cohabitation promotion. For too long, we have treated marriage as if it were a dreaded "M" word. Too afraid to say "marriage," we have instead talked about "committed relationships." But shacking up isn't getting married. Common sense says so. So does research. There is something fundamentally different about the commitment two people make within a marriage relationship versus a cohabiting relationship. In a cohabiting relationship, the commitment of each of the partners primarily is self-serving. By contrast, the marriage commitment is about serving one's spouse. This is a fundamental difference, and one that ought to be reflected in our social policy.

I recommend the following principles for government marriage promotion:

Government must resolve that it will not merely be "neutral" about marriage. For many behaviors government is rightly neutral, for others it is not. For example, the government is not neutral about home ownership because it is good for communities when people own their homes. Furthermore, the government is not neutral about charitable giving because charitable giving is good for society. In the same way, government should not be neutral about healthy marriages because they contribute directly to the general strength of a good and sound society.

Married Families Enjoy Higher Living Standards

Married families fare better, even toward bottom of income distribution

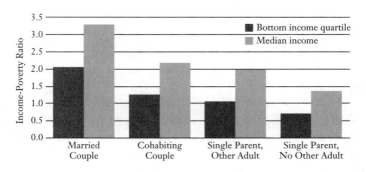

Tabulations from the 1999 National Survey of America's Families.

First of all, we must remove disincentives for marriage. Under current law if couples (especially low-income couples) marry, our tax code and social welfare system punish them. But striking these disincentives from our laws and policies, while a very important first step, only will bring us to the state of being neutral on marriage. We must go beyond that, into active support of marriage.

More than 90 percent of adults in the United States marry at some point during their lifetimes, and the vast majority enter marriage believing it to be a lifetime commitment. Surveys consistently document that most Americans see marriage as an important life goal. Clearly, providing active support for couples who want to marry and stay married is consistent with the values of the vast majority of Americans.

In doing so, government must not be paralyzed by the unknown. What we don't know about marriage promotion cannot be allowed to stand in the way of what we do know. Some have argued that we don't know enough about marriage promotion and, therefore, we should do nothing. They are partially correct. We have much to learn about promoting and supporting healthy marriages. But there is much we do know.

Premarital Education Should Be Encouraged

For example, thanks to a nascent marriage movement in our country, we do know that premarital-education programs work. We know that programs that assign mentoring couples to newlyweds do work. We know that good marriages are a result not of luck or chance but hard work and skill. We know that these skills can be taught. Finally, we know that programs designed to save even the most troubled marriages do work. Yes, there still is much to be learned, but we know enough about what works that standing by and doing nothing would be a tragic mistake.

New research constantly is shedding more light on our path. For example, research is debunking the myth that low-income, inner-city men and women who have children out of wedlock are not linked romantically and have no interest in marriage. A recent study by researchers at Princeton and Columbia universities revealed that 48 percent of unmarried urban couples were living together at the time their child was born. Eighty percent were involved in an exclusive romantic relationship. And half believed their chances of marrying—not at sometime to somebody, but to each other—were "certain" or "near certain." In other words, drive-by pregnancies are an especially insidious urban legend.

Now that we understand the goal for marriage promotion—helping couples who choose marriage develop the skills they need to build healthy marriages—it is time to explore specific actions the government can take. A number of proposals have been put forth. Here are five of my favorites—ideas that have the best chance of improving child well-being by strengthening the institution of marriage:

Five Steps That Promote Marriage

• Put marriage in the hospital. Hospitals should do more than talk about paternity establishment. They can talk about marriage as well. In most cases, hospital personnel stop at telling a young man that he must establish paternity. Doing so is extremely important. But hospital personnel should also ask the simple question, "Have you considered getting married?" If the answer is "yes," the couple can be referred to helpful services, such as premarital education. If the answer is "no," that's fine. But we can't be afraid to say the "M" word in the labor and delivery ward.

• Develop a referral system for premarital education. Schools, clinics, job-training sites and welfare offices all offer opportunities to provide referrals to premarital education.

• Provide marital-enrichment services through social programs dedicated to strengthening families. Head Start provides a perfect example. Many children in Head Start live with a married mother and father. While Head Start centers routinely provide parenting-education classes, I don't know of a single Head Start program providing marriage-education classes. Head Start represents a perfect opportunity to teach parents the skills they need to maintain a long-term, healthy marriage. We should seize this and similar opportunities.

• Create public-education campaigns highlighting the benefits of healthy marriages. The government funds numerous public-education campaigns promoting various healthy behaviors. Marriage can and should be added to this list.

• Increase support for intervention services, including mentoring programs, so that troubled marriages can be made whole and strong once again.

It no longer is a question of whether government should do this, but of how. It's time to get started right away, before another generation of children misses out on the benefits of a married mom and dad.

> "*Marriage-promotion policies provide a justification for growing inequality by implying that poverty is an individual pathology, a matter of personal failure.*"

Promoting Marriage Will Not Help End Poverty

Jeanne Winner

The marriage prescription that the George W. Bush administration is implementing offers no real assistance to poor people, argues Jeanne Winner in the following viewpoint. In Winner's view, people are not poor because they are unmarried but because the wages of low-income workers have steadily declined in the past thirty years. According to Winner, promoting marriage as a panacea to poverty encourages middle-class Americans to ignore the erosion of safety net benefits and instead blame the poor for their own declining standard of living. Jeanne Winner is a member of the *Dollars and Sense* collective, publishers of *Dollars and Sense* magazine.

As you read, consider the following questions:
1. According to the author, what is the message that marriage promotion delivers to poor people?
2. Why do the poor not consider marriage an easy way out of poverty, in Winner's opinion?
3. Why does Winner argue that having married parents is no guarantee that a child will escape poverty?

Jeanne Winner, "Should This Marriage Be Encouraged?" *Dollars and Sense*, November/December 2002, pp. 11–13. Copyright © 2002 by *Dollars and Sense*, a progressive economics magazine. www.dollarsandsense.org. Reproduced by permission.

Do George W. Bush and many members of Congress really believe that Cinderella is not just a fairy tale, but a policy brief for poor women? Encouraging marriage, Bush told the press [in] February [2002], is a key part of his program for reducing poverty among children—seven million of whom live with their single mothers below the poverty line in the United States. "My administration will give unprecedented support to strengthening marriage," he said. "Strong marriages and stable families are incredibly good for children." Senator Evan Bayh (D-Ind.) waxed even more enthusiastic on the social benefits of marriage: "If you're talking about breaking the cycle of poverty, this is one of the best things you can do."

Bill Clinton made the same claims for marriage when he was president. The 1996 welfare reform law he championed made "marriage promotion" an official part of federal welfare policy. Now, as part of the current reauthorization of that law, the Bush administration wants to divert an additional $300 million away from providing cash payments, health coverage, and child care assistance to poor families and into marriage promotion, or what critics call "wedfare," instead. And the administration is pressuring states to skirt welfare regulations in order to shift even more money into wedfare—in this case, funds intended for enforcement of child support. Wayne Horn, Assistant Secretary of Health and Human Services, has recommended pre-marital counseling, couples counseling, and even financial incentives to encourage marriage.

But for all his talk about ending poverty for children—which would have to mean ending it for parents as well—the president has found a way to take the high moral tone without spending any money. The marriage prescription offers no real assistance. It frames poverty as an individual choice and a personal responsibility: Economic conditions—like low-wage jobs—have nothing to do with it. Government policies that cut funds for housing, health care, and other supports for low-income workers have nothing to do with it. A tax system that favors the rich has nothing to do with it. The Bush and Clinton administrations have enjoined poor women to build strong families and marriages because of the value they bring to society. In the end, the message to poor people, and especially to women on welfare, is, "You provide the values. We'll keep the money."

Is Marriage the Answer?

Apart from the question of values, the arithmetic appears simple: Two incomes are greater than one. One household is cheaper to maintain than two. And two parents working together have more time and energy to take care of their children. Economic statistics give some support for the argument: in 2001 only 6.9% of married couples with children lived below the poverty line, but 35.1% of single mothers did.

With numbers like these, why aren't poor Americans rushing to marry, following their president's advice on how to improve their lot? The decisions of the poor confirm what many studies have found: Marriage is difficult and risky if you are poor. First, to escape poverty, it's not enough for poor men and women just to marry. They have to marry the right person, someone better off than they are. If they don't, the conditions of poverty—decaying neighborhoods, discrimination, poor health care, not enough money—will continue to place a great deal of stress on their relationships. Economic hardship can end a marriage. Divorce, for instance, rises as the unemployment rate rises; according to sociologist Scott South, 10,000 more couples divorce for each percentage point rise in the unemployment rate.

Marriage Offers No Guarantees

So, many women (and men) are not poor because they're unmarried—but they may be unmarried because they're poor. Furthermore, having married parents is no guarantee that a child will escape poverty. Many other factors can keep families in poverty—or lift them out of it. For example, getting a bachelor's degree dramatically reduces the poverty rate among single mothers—to 9.8% in 2001.

Wedfare policies are also likely to coerce women into bad or even abusive marriages. Putting aside what this means for women themselves, there are a host of studies on the damaging effects of difficult marriages on children. In fact, perhaps due to these effects, some studies of African-American children have found that children from single-parent homes show higher educational achievement than children from two-parent homes. "Are they going to give discounts on divorce when they promote marriage?" a Connecticut woman asked a *New York Times* reporter. She had left an abusive husband and had good reason to ask.

What's the Real Agenda?

All the talk about marriage diverts attention from the economic decisions the federal government has made about programs for low-income Americans, especially women. The average welfare benefit, never particularly generous, peaked in value in 1977 and had fallen 33% in real terms by 1995. Between 1994 and 1999, cash benefits for women on welfare fell about 11% further. In the late 1990s, the economic boom helped poor women survive, but it was not enough to protect growing numbers of women and children from hunger and homelessness. For example, in New Jersey, according to a 1999 report, 50.3% of former welfare recipients who were not in the labor force—and nearly 50% of those who were—could not feed themselves and their children adequately.

Economics Are Important to the Success of a Marriage

If married people are more likely (other things being equal) to produce thriving children, other things are not, in fact, equal. It's not just the case that single mothers find themselves poor because they are unmarried; they find themselves unmarried because they are poor. Successful marriages are more difficult when husbands and wives are poorly educated, lack access to jobs that pay decently, and cannot afford decent child care. Economic hardship and other problems associated with poverty can wreak havoc on couples' relationships.

Theodora Ooms, *American Prospect*, April 8, 2002.

Dismantling welfare is only part of the story, though. It's not only women receiving welfare who have seen their incomes decline in the past thirty years. Welfare recipients are one part of the larger corps of low-wage workers whose incomes have fallen as well. Consider those in minimum-wage jobs: at $5.15 an hour, the minimum wage is worth 24% less in real buying power today than it was in 1979. Middle-income Americans have likewise experienced growing economic insecurity; more than 60% of Americans have seen their real incomes fall since the 1970s. Only during the boom of the late 1990s did real incomes rise for this majority—but not enough to bring them back to where they'd been twenty-five years earlier. And between 1983 and 1998, the net worth of the poorest 40% of U.S. households *fell* by 76% while the net worth of the wealthiest 20% of households *rose* by 30%.

Poverty Equals Personal Failure

Overall, economic inequality has risen steadily over the past three decades. Where does wedfare fit in? Marriage-promotion policies provide a justification for growing inequality by implying that poverty is an individual pathology, a matter of personal failure. This view encourages middle-class Americans to be indifferent to the erosion of the social safety net. It diverts the public's attention away from decades of cuts in hard-won government programs for income security. From Ronald Reagan on, politicians have claimed that welfare programs cost too much. Since most Americans did not see any of the gains from the U.S. economy's recent expansion, they're susceptible to the idea that too many of their tax dollars are going to welfare recipients—that welfare recipients are somehow to blame for their own falling standard of living.

That's not true. But the very poor do hold up a mirror—dramatic and stark—to the economic insecurity that many Americans are experiencing. Government programs that provided poor people with greater income support would benefit most Americans. Such programs would set an income floor for all workers; give employees more power in the labor market; and make it clear that in such a complicated economy, we are dependent on one another and rely on each other's well-being for our own. But wedfare—in conjunction with cuts in welfare and other domestic programs—conveys the opposite message, both directly to the poor and implicitly to everyone else: "You're on your own."

Periodical Bibliography

The following articles have been selected to supplement the diverse views presented in this chapter.

Heather Boushey	"The Needs of the Working Poor: Helping Working Families Make Ends Meet," U.S. Senate, Committee on Health, Education, Labor and Pensions, February 14, 2002. www.senate.gov.
Thomas E. Buckley	"Church, State and the Faith-Based Initiative," *America*, November 11, 2002.
BusinessWeek Online	"Do 'Living Wages' Kill Business?" October 29, 2001.
Thomas J. DiLorenzo	"Reinventing America's Poor," *Free Market*, January 2000.
Dan Feder	"Work First—Where Are the Wages?" *Dollars and Sense*, November/December 2002.
Grocer	"Pay Rise Must Heed North-South Divide," July 20, 2002.
Fred Kammer	"Ending Poverty as We Know It," *Catholic Commentator*, November 15, 2000.
Josh Karp	"Higher Minimum Wage Wouldn't Be a Low Blow; Firms Say Paying More Is Worthwhile," *Crain's Chicago Business*, January 8, 2001.
Robert I. Lerman	"Should Government Promote Healthy Marriages?" *Urban Institute Short Takes on Welfare Policy*, May 31, 2002.
Ed Mayne and Gene Lender	"Should the Minimum Wage Increase by $1.00/Hour? (Up Front)," *Utah Business*, January 2002.
Theodora Ooms	"Marriage Plus: Most People Agree That It's Healthy for Kids to Grow Up in a Two-Parent Family. But the Marriage Contract Is Just the Beginning," *American Prospect*, April 8, 2002.
Kim Phillips-Fein	"The Education of Jessica Rivera: Trading in Their Books for Buckets, Welfare Recipients Learn 'Responsibility,'" *Nation*, November 25, 2002.
Joseph M. Sullivan	"Bush's Faith-Based Initiative: Worth a Serious Try?" *America*, April 9, 2001.

Adam Thomas and Isabel Sawhill	"For Richer or for Poorer: Marriage as an Antipoverty Strategy," *Brookings Institution Works in Progress*, May 2002.
Urban Institute	"Wedding Bells Ring in Stability and Economic Gains for Mothers and Children," September 5, 2002.
Gerald Wicz	"Libertarian Solutions: A Real Solution for Homelessness: Private Charity and Responsibility," *LP News*, February 1999.

CHAPTER 4

Is Worldwide Poverty a Serious Problem?

Chapter Preface

The impact of HIV/AIDS on poor nations is catastrophic. Nowhere is this tragedy more evident than in the forty-two nations that comprise the region known as sub-Saharan Africa. It is estimated that sub-Saharan Africa will have 71 million fewer people by 2010 than it would have had without the devastation of AIDS. The Joint United Nations Program on HIV/AIDS (UNAIDS) estimates that 36.1 million people worldwide are infected with HIV; 26 million of them live in Africa. South Africa is believed to have the highest percentage of HIV-infected adults in the world—25 percent are living with the disease. The South African government reports almost fifteen hundred new HIV infections a day and expects the death toll to reach 1 million by 2008.

Economic growth in Africa has been slowed significantly by AIDS. Estimates from the 1990s show that the virus reduced per capita annual growth by .8 percent. In African countries where the epidemic is worst, models suggest that 1 to 2 percentage points per capita will be lost in coming years. Further, after two decades, many economies will be 20 to 40 percent smaller than they would have been without the devastation of AIDS. AIDS-related illnesses and deaths that claim the majority of victims in their most productive working years—ages twenty to fifty—are exacerbating the poverty rampant in Africa. According to business experts, if the HIV/AIDS epidemic is not slowed, companies will have to train three people for every job, gambling that one will stay healthy long enough to be productive.

AIDS has been especially devastating to children living in developing nations. Sub-Saharan Africa has a total of 600,000 children under fifteen living with HIV/AIDS, according to a United Nations Population Fund report. Further, the deaths of young working adults—most of them parents— means an increase in the number of dependent orphans living in poverty. Children who have lost one or both parents to the disease—especially girls—are much less likely to continue their education either because they now lack the money or are needed at home to care for younger children or sick relatives. Moreover, the educational infrastructure in Africa is crumbling because there is no one to replace trained teachers and administrators as they succumb to the virus. In Kenya the death toll among teachers rose from 450 in 1995 to 1,400 in 1999. In the Central African Republic, 85 percent of the teachers who died between 1996 and 1998 were HIV-positive.

In addition to destroying the futures of Africa's children, the epidemic sweeping through southern Africa has exacerbated famine conditions in Lesotho, Malawi, Mozambique, Swaziland, Zambia, and Zimbabwe. According to *AIDS Epidemic Update 2002*, a report issued by UNAIDS and the World Health Organization (WHO), more than 5 million HIV/AIDS-infected adults (out of a total of 26 million) live in these six primarily agricultural countries. An AIDS-related death in a household that depends on farming can cause crop output to drop by as much as 60 percent. When a household suffers a labor loss due to illness, total income shrinks, leaving less money to buy food. "The famine is a tragic example of how this epidemic combines with other crises to create even greater catastrophes. . . . Responses to AIDS must take into account that the epidemic has an impact in every economic and social sector," said Dr. Peter Piot, executive director of UNAIDS. "The famine in southern Africa brings the world face-to-face with the deep and devastating impact of AIDS," he said.

The link between poverty and HIV/AIDS in Africa and the rest of the world is indisputable. Authors in the following chapters examine the relationship between poverty and other global phenomena, such as terrorism, globalization, increased population, and genetic engineering.

*"The war on terrorism won't succeed
without a war on poverty."*

Global Poverty Causes Terrorism

Strobe Talbott

In the following viewpoint, Strobe Talbott argues that poverty, hunger, and ill health create despair in those who consider themselves losers in the process of globalization and modernization. Such desperation results in anger, hatred, and ultimately terrorism against those they perceive as winners. He contends that while suicide bombers are usually privileged and well educated, their constituencies are the poor who feel victimized. Talbott maintains that only when the United States helps end the poverty that terrorist leaders exploit will terrorism end. Strobe Talbott is director of the Yale Center for the Study of Globalization.

As you read, consider the following questions:
1. According to the author, which way is the scale tipping—toward the winners or toward the losers?
2. What does Talbott say is the best way to address the poverty that terrorists exploit?
3. What is Congress writing a blank check for, in the author's opinion?

Strobe Talbott, "The Other Evil," *Foreign Policy*, November/December 2001, p. 75. Copyright © 2001 by Foreign Policy Magazine. Reproduced by permission.

T he war on terrorism won't succeed without a war on poverty.

History has often boiled down to the word versus: Athens versus Sparta, Rome versus Carthage, Imperial Britain versus Napoleonic France or Czarist Russia. For most of the second half of the 20th century, the Great Versus was capitalism versus communism. During the first decade after the end of the Cold War, there were hints (sometimes gruesome and portentous, as in the Balkans and Africa) of what was coming next: the forces of integration versus those of disintegration; the effort to build a New World Order—a still-serviceable catchphrase from Bush I [George Bush, father of George W. Bush]—versus the New Jihad, with its implicit doctrine of "worse is better" and its celebration of mayhem and slaughter.

Underlying the long-term challenge of the post-September 11 [2001, terrorist attacks on America], era is much more than Islamic defiance of the Great Satan. There is a growing divide between what we've traditionally thought of as the haves and the have-nots, but who might better be described as those who feel like winners in the process of globalization and modernization and those who feel like losers.

There are about 6 billion people on the earth today. About half of them are struggling to survive on less than $2 a day and have never seen a personal computer or, for that matter, ever made a telephone call. That fifty-fifty ratio is unstable. It's tipping in the wrong direction in two respects: The numbers of poor are growing faster than the numbers of rich, and the gap between rich and poor is widening. When self-perceived losers outnumber self-perceived winners, it's lose-lose for everyone.

The Victims Become the Victimizers

We must distinguish between, on the one hand, the assassins and those who mastermind and abet their operations and, on the other hand, their constituencies—those millions who feel so victimized by the modern world that they want us to be victims, too; those who see [terrorist] Osama bin Laden as a combination avenging angel and Robin Hood. As the mug shots and bios of the suicide pilots emerged, it became apparent that for the most part they did not come from the ranks of the world's desperate and aggrieved. Their fanaticism, like bin Laden's, was nurtured in privilege and in individual madness. During the immediate aftermath of the attacks on New York and Washington, the focus has rightly been on that species of menace, difficult to fathom, find, or deter, yet utterly deserving eradication.

Poverty Fuels Terrorism

A strategy that pins our fate to a war on terrorism backed by excessive consumption in America—or anywhere else for that matter—will ultimately blow up in our faces. A war on poverty, on the other hand, can and must be won.

David Ransom, *New Internationalist*, November 2001.

However, the other set of images so memorable from September 11—Palestinians and Pakistanis dancing in the streets—is a reminder of a parallel challenge. Disease, overcrowding, undernourishment, political repression, and alienation breed despair, anger, and hatred. These are the raw materials of what we're up against, and they constitute a check on the willingness of Arab and other regimes to take effective action against networks of conspirators.

The principal way to address those conditions is through economic aid, refugee relief, public health campaigns, democracy promotion, and diplomacy as the first line of defense against communal and regional conflict. There will have to be not only more international development assistance but also better strategies for making the money work. That, in itself, will require urgent and concerted rethinking and reform. Throwing money at good causes has too often lined the pockets of bureaucrats and politicians—and not only in the countries receiving foreign aid. Traditional approaches must be supplemented, and in some cases replaced, by innovative ones, such as microcredit projects and programs aimed at empowering women as a force for social, economic, and political advancement.

Foreign Aid Must Be Increased

In addition to rethinking and reform, there will have to be vastly increased commitments from treasuries, first and foremost that of the United States.

Yet exactly the opposite seems to be in prospect.

Programs that are instrumental in getting at the roots of terrorism are more in jeopardy now than they were two months ago. The blank check that Congress seems willing to write is for enhancing military defenses (including a national anti-missile system), improving intelligence-gathering and covert action, keeping airlines in business, and reinforcing airport and onboard security.

The United States will throw itself into meeting those priorities just as the nation says goodbye to its hard-won surplus and heads into what threatens to be a severe recession. In the budget crunch ahead, there will be a temptation to squeeze down the very programs that will allow us to move from reactive, defensive warfare against the terrorists to a proactive, prolonged offensive against the ugly, intractable realities that terrorists exploit and from which they derive popular support, foot soldiers, and political cover. That's why another phrase from America's political past needs to be dusted off, put back in service, and internationalized: the war on poverty. Only if the long struggle ahead is also fought on that front will it be winnable.

"Reducing poverty is not an answer [to reducing terrorism]."

Global Poverty Does Not Cause Terrorism

Jane R. Eisner

In the following viewpoint, Jane R. Eisner contends that terrorists are not motivated by poverty, desperation, and an overwhelming need to improve their living conditions. Rather, she maintains, they are driven by the religious and political fanaticism that thrives in countries without democratic traditions or infrastructures. She argues that despite wealth derived from oil and a relatively high standard of living, Arab countries foster terrorism because they are crippled by a lack of political freedom, the repression of women, and isolation from creative ideas and culture. Jane R. Eisner is a columnist for the *Philadelphia Inquirer.*

As you read, consider the following questions:

1. What does Eisner say are the twin tools of American success?
2. In the author's opinion, terrorism is not an economic crime. What is it?
3. According to Eisner, the Arab region scores the lowest in the world on which index?

Jane R. Eisner, "Terrorism's Tenuous Link to Poverty," *Knight Ridder/Tribune News Service,* July 8, 2002, p. K-1003. Copyright © 2002 by Tribune Media Services. Reproduced by permission.

"We fight against poverty," President George W. Bush said recently, "because hope is an answer to terror." Terrorism will not be defeated, World Bank President James Wolfensohn says repeatedly, unless world poverty is eradicated.

To our Western minds and pocketbooks, where money is the motivation for everything and poverty a niggling blot on our consciences, terrorism must be linked to poverty. Who else but the poor and uneducated would be desperate enough to kill innocent people and terrorize millions of others, or support those who commit such horrible crimes? Only the ones left in a heap at the bottom of society, with nothing else to lose, would hijack airplanes, detonate suicide bombs or attempt to destroy civilization's foundations.

And therefore economic opportunity and education—the twin tools of American success—are the antidote to terror, the vaccine against this virulent, modern disease. Raise income levels, improve the standard of living, put money in the pockets of Third World citizens and food on their tables and they won't turn themselves into weapons of mass destruction.

Or so the reasoning goes.

But there's another argument gaining adherents among those who spend their time trying to pinpoint the precise "root causes" of terrorism, and it should interest the rest of us who pay the price and foot the bill for anti-terror efforts.

Terrorists Are Motivated by Religious and Political Fanaticism

In fact, terrorists draw their support and their human ammunition not from the most impoverished, illiterate in their societies, but from the educated and (relatively) well-off. In fact, terrorists are not motivated by a desperate, ill-informed attempt to improve living conditions but by religious and political fanaticism bred in countries without democratic infrastructures.

Terrorism isn't an economic crime; it's a violent form of political engagement. And this understanding, says Princeton economist Alan B. Krueger, should lead the West to very different solutions than the ones promoted now.

"We should be helping to bring in more democracy and develop dissent in non-violent ways," Krueger says. "Reducing poverty is not an answer."

Krueger and Jitka Maleckova, a Mideast expert at Charles University in Prague, came to this conclusion after analyzing several pieces of evidence. They pored over newspaper stories about 129 members of the terrorist organization Hezbollah in Lebanon who died in action, mostly against Israel, from 1982 to 1994 and found that the terrorists were, on average, more educated and less impoverished than the Lebanese population.

The Connection Between Poverty and Terrorism Is False

Drawing a false and unjustified connection between poverty and terrorism is potentially quite dangerous, as the international aid community may lose interest in providing support to developing nations when the imminent threat of terrorism recedes, much as support for development waned in the aftermath of the Cold War; and connecting foreign aid with terrorism risks the possibility of humiliating many people in less developed countries, who are implicitly told that they receive aid only to prevent them from committing acts of terror. Moreover, premising foreign aid on the threat of terrorism could create perverse incentives in which some groups are induced to engage in terrorism to increase their prospects of receiving aid. In our view, alleviating poverty is reason enough to pressure economically advanced countries to provide more aid than they are currently giving. Falsely connecting terrorism to poverty serves only to deflect attention from the real roots of terrorism.

Alan B. Krueger and Jitka Maleckova, *New Republic Online*, June 24, 2002.

They made a similar analysis of 27 Israeli Jewish extremists who committed terrorist acts in the early 1980s and found that they, too, were overwhelmingly well-educated and in high-paying occupations.

Terrorism Is a Form of Revolutionary Violence

Most persuasively, they studied several years of polling of Palestinian public opinion and found that support for suicide bombers was "strongest among the better-educated, the merchants and professionals." The illiterate and unemployed were the least supportive.

Beyond these actual studies, there's plenty of anecdotal evidence to debunk the link between poverty and terrorism. Look no further than Spain and Ireland—two relatively affluent nations struck repeatedly by terror—or for that matter, [the 1995 bombing of the Federal Building in] Oklahoma City, Oklahoma. As Michael Radu of the Foreign Policy Research Institute, wrote recently: "Ever since the Russian intellectuals 'invented' modern terrorism in the 19th century, revolutionary violence—terrorism is just one form of it—has been a virtual monopoly of the relatively privileged. Terrorists have been middle class, often upper class, and always educated, but never poor."

The well-schooled, well-heeled hijackers on Sept. 11, 2001, then, were not the exception but the rule.

And although terrorism is not restricted to one region or nationality, a fascinating report issued in Cairo helps explain why it has taken root so dangerously in the Arab world. The report—compiled by Arab intellectuals and commissioned by the United Nations—warns that Arab societies are being crippled by a lack of political freedom, the repression of women and a dramatic isolation from creative ideas and culture.

This despite the fact that the standard of living in Arab countries has advanced considerably. Life expectancy is longer than the world average, the level of abject poverty is the world's lowest and infant mortality has sharply declined in recent decades.

Supporting Democracy Is More Important than Ending Poverty

Nevertheless, productivity is declining, science and technology are dormant, research and development are weak or nonexistent. The entire Arab world—22 nations, 280 million people—translates about 330 books annually, one-fifth the number that little Greece translates each year.

And as if to underscore Krueger's message, the region scores the lowest in the world on a standard freedom index, which measures civil liberties, government accountability, political rights and media freedom. Even sub-Saharan Africa, with its searing poverty, offers its citizens more freedom and—not coincidentally—produces fewer terrorists.

Supporting democracy in non-Western cultures is a delicate, risky task. But . . . it is one we should embrace with renewed passion.

"Globalization holds the most promise for developing countries with respect to economic growth, poverty reduction, and the reversal of global inequality."

Globalization Is Helping to Reduce World Poverty

Ian Vásquez

In the following viewpoint, Ian Vásquez argues that globalization offers the world's poor a shortcut out of poverty. He contends that globalization will allow today's developing countries to recreate the dramatic economic advances that Western countries experienced in the early nineteenth century. Further, he maintains, the intense, sustained economic growth that has occurred in developed countries in the past two hundred years can only take place in an environment that encourages free enterprise and the protection of private property. Ian Vásquez is the director of the Project on Global Economic Liberty at the Cato Institute, a libertarian research foundation.

As your read, consider the following questions:

1. According to Vásquez, what advantage do today's developing countries have?
2. The Fraser study found that economic freedom is strongly related to what, in the author's opinion?
3. In the author's opinion, which three institutional reforms are most important to the poor?

Ian Vásquez, "Globalization and the Poor," *The Independence Review*, vol. 12, Fall 2002, pp. 197–206. Copyright © 2002 by The Independent Institute, 100 Swan Way, Oakland, CA 94621-1428, USA; info@independent.org, www.independent.org. Reproduced by permission.

Globalization holds the most promise for developing countries with respect to economic growth, poverty reduction, and the reversal of global inequality. Most important, globalization is helping parts of the developing world to replicate the experience that Western countries went through beginning around 1820, when they broke with the historical norm of low growth and initiated an era of dramatic advances in material well-being. Living standards tripled in Europe and quadrupled in the United States in the nineteenth century, and they improved at an even faster pace in the twentieth century. Economic growth thus eliminated mass poverty in what is today considered the developed world.

The West's escape from poverty did not occur by chance. Sustained growth over long periods of time took place in an environment that generally encouraged free enterprise and the protection of private property. Today, developing countries have an advantage. By adopting liberal economic policies, they can achieve within one generation the kind of economic progress that rich countries took a hundred years to achieve. Rapid growth is possible because poor countries will be catching up to rich countries rather than breaking a new path.

Economic Freedom and Prosperity Are Strongly Linked

The most comprehensive empirical study of the relationship between economic policies and prosperity is the Fraser Institute's annual report *Economic Freedom of the World*, copublished by the Cato Institute. It examines more than twenty components of economic freedom, ranging from size of government to monetary and trade policy, in 123 countries over a twenty-five-year period. The study finds a strong relationship between economic freedom and prosperity. With the countries divided by quintiles, the freest economies have an average income per capita of $19,800 compared with $2,210 in the least-free quintile. Freer economies also grow faster than less-free economies. Annual growth of output per capita in the 1990s was 2.27 percent in the freest quintile, but—1.45 percent in the least-free countries.

The Fraser study also found that economic freedom is

strongly related to poverty reduction. The United Nations Human Poverty Index, for example, is negatively correlated with the Fraser index of economic freedom. The recent acceleration of growth in many developing countries indeed has reduced poverty, measured as those living on less than one dollar a day. In the past ten years in the developing world, the percentage of people who are poor fell from 29 to 24 percent. Despite that progress, however, the number of poor people has remained stubbornly high at approximately 1.2 billion, and reductions in poverty have been uneven geographically.

This mixed performance has prompted many observers . . . to ask what factors other than growth reduce poverty and whether growth is enough to accomplish that goal. Market reforms themselves have been questioned as a way of helping the poor. After all, many developing countries have liberalized their economies to varying degrees in the past decade.

Economic Growth Equals Poverty Reduction

The pattern of poverty reduction we see around the world should not be surprising. It generally follows the relationship found by a recent World Bank study that considered growth in sixty-five developing countries during the 1980s and 1990s. The share of people in poverty, defined as those living on less than one dollar per day, almost always declined in countries that experienced growth and increased in countries that experienced economic contractions. The faster the growth, the study found, the faster the poverty reduction and vice versa. For example, an increase in income per capita of 8.2 percent translated into a 6.1 reduction in the poverty rate. A contraction of 1.9 percent in output led to an increase of 1.5 percent in the poverty rate.

That relationship explains why some countries and regions have done better than others. "Between 1987 and 1998, there was only one region of the world that saw a dramatic fall in both the number of people and the proportion of the population living on less than a dollar a day. That region was East Asia," observes economist Martin Wolf. "But this was also the only region to see consistent and rapid growth in real incomes per head. . . ."

The growth induced by globalization does not just reduce

poverty. The Fraser Institute study found that economic freedom is related strongly to other indicators of progress. For example, people living in the top 20 percent of countries in terms of economic freedom tend to live approximately two decades longer than people in the bottom 20 percent. Lower infant mortality, higher literacy rates, less corruption, and greater access to safe drinking water are also associated with increases in economic liberty. Indeed, the United Nations Human Development Index, which measures various aspects of standards of living, correlates positively with greater economic freedom.

Globalizing Countries Have Higher Growth Rates

The empirical evidence also shows that critics of globalization are wrong about the effects of global capitalism on inequality, both within and among countries. A recent World Bank study, for example, compared the performance of globalizing and nonglobalizing developing countries. It found that globalizing countries had higher growth rates (approximately 5 percent in the 1990s) than other countries, rich or poor. Countries participating in globalization thus are catching up with rich countries. Because the high-growth countries include China and India, which contain half of the developing world's poor, the growth in global inequality that had occurred for some two hundred years is now ending, and perhaps global inequality has begun to decline.

Consistent with other studies, the World Bank report also found that globalization has not increased inequality within nations. In some countries, inequality has risen, in others it has not, but liberalization has had no general effect on changes in income shares. In general, the incomes of the poorest 20 percent of the population in liberalizing countries have risen proportionately with the average rise in income. Because many countries are making the transition from socialism to the market, moreover, the increase in inequality should not be surprising or alarming. Anders Aslund shows, for example, that in the fast-reforming countries of the former Soviet bloc, inequality has risen to western European levels, whereas among the gradual reformers inequality has grown to U.S. levels.

The Neglected Agenda

Although the collapse of central planning forced many countries to abandon inward-looking economic policies in the 1990s, most of the developing world is still far from adopting a coherent set of policies consistent with economic freedom. Russia may have dumped communism, but in terms of economic freedom the Fraser Institute ranks it 117 out of 123 nations. Even countries such as Argentina and Mexico that have done much to liberalize their economies have clung to policy remnants of the past, with devastating consequences for the poor. Mexico's peso crisis of 1994–95, for example, resulted from monetary and fiscal policies during an election year that were thoroughly inconsistent with market economics.

Attention to market-oriented macroeconomic policies is well founded, particularly because they benefit the poor. This point applies especially to two such policies that disproportionately favor the poor—reducing inflation and reducing government spending. Much less attention, however, has been paid to institutional reforms and the microeconomic environment. Although the reform agenda in most countries is quite long, three areas stand out: the rule of law, the extent of bureaucratic regulation, and the private-property rights of the poor.

Globalization Is Not New

Globalization is not just a recent phenomenon. Some analysts have argued that the world economy was just as globalized 100 years ago as it is today. But today commerce and financial services are far more developed and deeply integrated than they were at that time. The most striking aspect of this has been the integration of financial markets made possible by modern electronic communication.

International Monetary Fund Issues Brief, April 12, 2000.

A legal system capable of enforcing contracts and protecting persons and their property rights in an evenhanded manner is central to both economic freedom and progress. Indeed, the sustainability of a market economy—and of market reforms themselves—rests in large part on the application of the rule of law. Yet the rule of law is conspicuously missing in much of the developing world. . . .

The Rule of Law Is the Key to Economic Prosperity

The absence of the rule of law is especially unfortunate for the poor, not only because they have fewer private resources to protect their rights, but also because the rule of law in itself is related to economic growth. Robert Barro created an index that measures the rule of law on a scale of 0 to 6, and he found that a country's growth rate increases by half a percentage point with each increment in his index. Because the rule of law provides essential protections for the poor, sustains a market-exchange system, and promotes growth, it may well be the most important ingredient of economic prosperity.

Another much-neglected area in need of reform is regulation. Here again the Fraser Institute's comprehensive index shows that the freedom to operate a business and to compete in the market is circumscribed in much of the developing world. The same countries that rank low in the rule of law also rank low in this area. . . .

The informal economy in the developing world is large because of another major factor: the private-property rights of the poor are not recognized legally. Peruvian economist Hernando de Soto has documented how poor people around the world have no security in their assets because they lack legal title to their property. . . . Without secure private-property rights, the poor cannot use collateral to get a loan, cannot take out insurance, and find it difficult to plan for the long term. . . .

Extending the system of property-rights protection to include the property of poor people is the most important social reform that developing countries can undertake. It is a reform that has been ignored almost completely around the world, yet it would affect the poor directly and produce dramatic results for literally billions of people.

Globalization as a Bottom-Up Process

Both the enemies and the proponents of globalization often attribute the implementation of market policies to the guidance of international institutions such as the International Monetary Fund (IMF), the World Bank, or the United Nations, and both groups often recommend that further global developments be managed by international bodies.

Those views are unfortunate because they give the false impression that globalization is somehow imposed from above. In truth, the world economy has evolved as a result of changes coming from the national level rather than changes directed at the international level—what German liberal Wilhelm Röpke called an international order "from within and beneath" rather than the "false internationalism" that characterizes supranational organizations. Moreover, the constructivist approach to achieving a liberal economic world order is fraught with peril because it can have unintended consequences and may lead to discretionary and arbitrary use of power. . . .

Multilateral aid intended to reduce poverty and to promote market reforms, for example, in practice has reduced prosperity and slowed the move to world capitalism. IMF bailouts have created both moral hazard and the impression that capitalism somehow has failed. Official international organizations also have been used to pressure poor countries to adopt labor and environmental regulations that are inimical to growth and contrary to the wishes of developing countries and the vast majority of consumers in rich countries. Deepak Lal notes that the West's efforts to promote labor, environmental, and other standards in the developing world are reminiscent of nineteenth-century imperialism and its attempts to legislate its "habits of the heart" worldwide, which did so much to undermine that era's liberal economic order.

Capitalism Decreases Poverty and Global Inequality

Globalization is proving the antiglobalization movement wrong in the area that is perhaps its central feature: the spread of capitalism is reducing poverty and global inequality. This reduction is not enough, however, for liberals to dismiss as misinformed the claims of the antiglobalists in this area or in others. Liberals must take the offensive and occupy the moral high ground in the globalization debate rather than play a defensive role when crises break out (John Micklethwait and Adrian Wooldridge [2000] make much the same point). The task ahead is to show how all developing countries, including those that have done much to liberalize their economies, are still a long way from establishing free markets based on private-property rights and the rule of law. Our challenge is enormous because we can expect the ongoing process of globalization to be uneven and rough, nor is its outcome inevitable.

"Economic globalization is a cause of global poverty and inequality, not a solution."

Globalization Is Making World Poverty Worse

Antonia Jubasz

In the following viewpoint, Antonia Jubasz argues that globalization increases poverty and inequality because it encourages free trade, financial liberalization, deregulation, reduced government spending, and privatization—policies that concentrate wealth at the top and marginalize the poor. Further, she maintains that the economic and human costs of adjusting to increased market openness are borne almost exclusively by the poor, whether the adjustment is rapid or slow. Jubasz contends that due to globalism, poverty in developing countries has increased, not decreased, in the past decade. Antonia Jubasz is the project director of the International Forum on Globalization.

As you read, consider these questions:
1. According to Jubasz, how does President George W. Bush want to end terrorism?
2. In Jubasz's opinion, why is the U.S. government offering loans to Pakistan and Indonesia rather than direct aid?
3. Which segment of the U.S. population experienced large wealth gains since 1983, as reported by the author?

Antonia Jubasz, "The Globalization of Poverty," *Tikkun*, vol. 16, November/December 2001, p. 20. Copyright © 2001 by *Tikkun*. Reproduced by permission.

United States Trade Representative Robert Zoellick has begun to use the horrific tragedies of September 11, 2001 as a rationale to push an aggressive free trade agenda, arguing that we must "counter terrorism with trade." An expansive economic globalization agenda is one of the four policy priorities President George W. Bush asked Congress to address immediately following the attacks of September 11. The administration is arguing that we will end terrorism through trade because economic globalization is the solution to poverty. But all evidence shows the contrary, that economic globalization is a cause of global poverty and inequality, not a solution. Furthermore, this evidence is increasingly coming from within the institutions of economic globalization itself.

For example, the Central Intelligence Agency itself warned in a December 2000 report that economic globalization would increase inequality and poverty, thereby fostering violence: "The rising tide of the global economy will create many economic winners, but it will not lift all boats. . . . [It will] spawn conflicts at home and abroad, ensuring an even wider gap between regional winners and losers than exists today. . . . [Globalization's] evolution will be rocky, marked by chronic financial volatility and a widening economic divide. Regions, countries, and groups feeling left behind will face deepening economic stagnation, political instability, and cultural alienation. They will foster political, ethnic, ideological, and religious extremism, along with the violence that often accompanies it."

The most reliable data available, predominantly from supporters of economic globalization, demonstrate how economic globalization has caused the most dramatic increase in global inequality and poverty in modern history. Furthermore, this outcome is intrinsic to the economic globalization model. Arguments that economic globalization allows "fragile democracies" to "overcome poverty and create opportunity," as Trade Representative Zoellick wrote in the *Washington Post*, are seriously mistaken. If such policies are pursued, the world could find itself in even worse circumstances in the future than those we find ourselves in today.

The IMF Has Failed Miserably

The administration has already begun to move ahead with International Monetary Fund (IMF) loans to Pakistan and Indonesia in the name of fighting terrorism. If we wish to help these countries with their economic problems, why are we providing loans instead of direct aid? Why are we using the IMF, an institution that has failed miserably in this region (as former World Bank chief economist Joseph Stiglitz wrote, "All the IMF did was make East Asia's recessions deeper, longer, and harder.") instead of alternative funding sources, such as the United Nations, that historically represent the interests of developing countries? The answer may be that the U.S. government can control the funds that go to a country through the IMF by linking conditions to the loans. These conditions have historically benefited corporate and elite interests over those of the populations of the countries in question.

Globalisation Undermines Justice

Globalisation is the rule of commerce and it has elevated Wall Street to be the only source of value. As a result things that should have high worth—nature, culture, the future— are being devalued and destroyed. The rules of globalisation are undermining the rules of justice and sustainability, of compassion and sharing. We have to move from market totalitarianism to an earth democracy.

Vandana Shiva, *BBC Reith Lectures 2000*, May 13, 2000.

The CIA is not alone in its assessment of the catastrophic impact that the policies of economic globalization have had around the world. For example, the World Bank—one of economic globalization's leading institutions—reports that "Globalization appears to increase poverty and inequality. . . . The costs of adjusting to greater openness are borne exclusively by the poor, regardless of how long the adjustment takes."

The United Nations echoes these words in its 1999 *Human Development Report*, "The new rules of globalization— and the players writing them—focus on integrating global markets, neglecting the needs of people that markets cannot meet. The process is concentrating power and marginalizing the poor, both countries and people. . . . The current [globalization] debate is . . . too narrow . . . neglecting broader human concerns such as persistent global poverty, growing inequality between and within countries, exclusion of poor people and countries and persistent human rights abuses."

Globalization Concentrates Wealth at the Top

The policies of economic globalization such as free trade, financial liberalization, deregulation, reduced government spending, and privatization concentrate wealth at the top, removing from governments and communities the very tools needed to ensure equity and to protect workers, social services, the environment, and sustainable livelihoods. In this way, economic globalization and its institutions—including the International Monetary Fund (IMF), the World Bank, the World Trade Organization, and the North American Free Trade Agreement, have created the most dramatic increase in global inequality—both within and between nations—in modern history and have increased global poverty.

For example, the income gap between the fifth of the world's people living in the richest countries and the fifth in the poorest doubled from 1960 to 1990, from thirty to one to sixty to one. By 1998 it had jumped again, with the gap widening to an astonishing seventy-eight to one. Poverty trends have worsened as well; there are 100 million more poor people in developing countries today than a decade ago. The assets of the three richest people on earth are greater than the combined Gross National Product of the forty-eight least developed countries. Even in the United States, where median earnings of workers more than doubled from 1947 to 1973, the past two decades have seen median earnings fall by almost 15 percent, with the earnings for the poorest 20 percent of households falling the furthest behind. In fact, the only segment of the U.S. population that has experienced large wealth gains since 1983 is the richest 20 percent of households. The net worth of the top 1 percent of U.S. households now exceeds that of the bottom 90 percent.

As Professor Robert Wade of the London School of Economics wrote in *The Economist*, "Global inequality is worsening rapidly. . . . Technological change and financial liberalization result in a disproportionately fast increase in the number of households at the extreme rich end, without shrinking the distribution at the poor end. . . . From 1988 to 1993, the share of the world income going to the poorest 10 percent of the world's population fell by over a quarter, whereas the share of the richest 10 percent rose by 8 percent. The richest 10 percent pulled away from the median, while the poorest 10 percent fell away from the median, falling absolutely and by a large amount."

Globalization Serves Only the Rich

It is time to recognize that economic globalization does not serve the poor, it serves the wealthy. It actually adds to the numbers of poor while concentrating greater amounts of wealth among an ever-dwindling number of people. As Thabo Mbeki, the president of South Africa, said, "We believe consciousness is rising, including in the North, about the inequality and insecurity globalization has brought about the plight of poor countries."

For the U.S. Trade Representative to argue that expanding the World Trade Organization, signing the Free Trade Area of the Americas, and granting the President "Trade Promotion Authority" (formally Fast Track) to side-step Congress in the creation of national legislation will address the root problems of global instability is opportunistic, disrespectful, and cynical. It is time to reject failed models and embrace new alternatives.

5

"Slowing population growth aids development."

High Population Growth Is Exacerbating World Poverty

Population Reports

In the following viewpoint, the editors of *Population Reports* argue that economic development and the reduction of poverty are impossible if population growth goes unchecked. Slowing population growth, they maintain, allows greater governmental investments in education, heath care, sanitation, and housing, which, in the long run, work to reduce poverty. Further, couples with fewer children save more and increase domestic investment as well, which also helps eliminate poverty. The editors contend that government-supported family planning services are key to slowing population growth and decreasing poverty. *Population Reports* is a publication of the U.S. Health Department.

As you read, consider the following questions:
1. In the editors' opinion, how does development itself contribute to slower population growth?
2. Where do regions of the world with high population growth rates rank on the United Nations Human Development Index, according to the editors?
3. According to the editors, what developmental goal is closely linked to protecting the environment and slowing population growth?

"Aiding Development," *Population Reports*, vol. 27, July 1999, p. 20.

As couples have fewer children, population growth slows, providing a demographic bonus that countries can invest in better education, health care, job creation, and other improvements.

Slowing population growth aids development. Development requires making investments today to raise living standards tomorrow. But it is difficult to make such investments when resources are already fully used trying to keep up with the current needs of rapidly growing populations. When population growth slows, developing countries are better able to invest more per capita in education, health care, sanitation, and other productive improvements.

Development itself also contributes to slower population growth by leading couples to desire fewer children. Development by itself, however, can do little to reduce fertility levels and slow population growth. Family planning information and services also must be widely available and accessible so that couples can achieve their fertility desires.

Rapid population growth, unemployment, and lack of savings and investment are part of a cycle of poverty that trouble many developing countries. This cycle could be broken if governments at the same time emphasized providing family planning and stimulating economic growth.

In some countries living standards have improved after population growth slowed substantially. "Even in adverse circumstances—low incomes, limited education, and few opportunities for women—family planning programs have meant slower population growth and improved family welfare," the World Bank has noted.

Population and Economic Growth

In theory, population growth might provide an economic advantage because more people could be working, produce more, and thus raise national income levels. In reality, studies in many countries find that rapid population growth has resulted in more poverty for most people.

In fact, the regions of the world where fertility and population growth rates are the highest rank lowest on the United Nations Human Development Index.

When population growth is rapid, economies often cannot create enough jobs to go around. In developing countries 800 million people are unemployed or underemployed—more than the entire workforce of the industrialized world. These high-fertility countries must create 40 million new jobs each year just to keep even.

A study of 99 countries in 1994 found that population growth had little impact on growth of per capita output during the 1960s and 1970s. It had a strong negative impact in the 1980s, however. Rapid population growth may have become more difficult to accommodate at a time of world recession and net outflows of resources from developing countries to industrialized countries.

Other research has found that rapid population growth dampens economic growth. Gross domestic product (GDP)—the market value of all goods and services produced in a given time period—is a measure of the economic strength of a country. A study of GDP trends and population growth in 72 countries during 1968–74 and 1977–83 found that higher population growth slowed GDP growth in the short term. Another study of 82 countries found that in the 1980s average income per person grew 2.5% more per year in the 41 countries with the slowest population growth than in the 41 countries with the fastest population growth.

Greater Productivity Supports Social Improvements

When population growth slows, income per capita typically rises. For example, a study of 107 countries found that between 1960 and 1985 fertility declines consistently were followed by growth in per capita income. This boost in productivity and income results largely from a "demographic bonus"—a change in the age structure of the population. As population growth slows, there is a decline in the dependency ratio—the number of dependents relative to the number of working-age people.

Greater productivity typically generates higher earnings, more savings, and more investment per capita, which in turn can help support education, health care, and other social improvements that boost productivity further. This dynamic process has been identified as one of the key reasons that the economies of many Asian countries grew rapidly between 1960 and 1990.

Countries with rapid population growth often have high unemployment and low savings levels. Parents cannot afford to save, nor do they need to save because they rely on their children and extended family to help in emergencies, illness, and old age. As parents have fewer dependent children, their ability and their motivation to save increase.

Population Problems Increase

World population, now 6.1 billion, has doubled since 1960 and is projected to grow by half, to 9.3 billion, by 2050. Some 2 billion people already lack food security, and water supplies and agricultural lands are under increasing pressure. Water use has risen six-fold over the past 70 years; by 2050, 4.2 billion people will be living in countries that cannot meet people's daily basic needs.

US Newswire, November 5, 2001.

A higher savings rate leads to greater domestic investment and capital deepening—that is, an increase in the amount of capital relative to the number of workers in an economy. In contrast, when rates of savings and investment are low, economic growth can slow, or even decline, leading to stagnant or falling living standards. In sub-Saharan Africa, as domestic savings declined from 27% of GDP in 1980 to 15% in 1993, domestic investment dropped from 24% of GDP to 16%.

Countries with rapid population growth tend to spend less per child on education than those with slow population growth. In turn, declining education levels often lead to declines in productivity and to lower incomes.

In contrast, when fertility declines, school systems are able to educate a higher percentage of young people. As the educational level of the workforce rises, labor productivity often rises. An increase of one year in the average education of the labor force is associated with an increase of GDP of between 4% and 9%.

Toward Sustainable Development

Especially in countries where the population is growing rapidly, slowing this growth would go far to relieve pressures both on the economy and on the natural environment. Populations cannot continue to grow and consumption levels to rise indefinitely without the likelihood of some day despoiling the natural environment on which present and future generations depend.

Instead, the concept of sustainable development recognizes that the process of social and economic development can continue without sacrificing the environment. The effort requires a combination of wise public investment, effective natural resource management, cleaner agricultural and industrial technologies, less pollution, and slower population growth.

Better resource management protects the environment and preserves nature's productive capacity. Stronger economies can afford to invest more in protecting the environment. Slower population growth can speed economic growth and preserve natural resources.

Increasingly, development experts and environmentalists agree that efforts to improve living standards and protect the environment can be complementary. In fact, reducing poverty, protecting the environment, and slowing population growth are closely linked.

"Human beings . . . can progressively and intentionally augment the 'resource base' that sustains them."

The World Can Sustain Its Growing Population

Nicholas Eberstadt

In the following viewpoint, Nicholas Eberstadt argues that because human beings have an almost unlimited ability to expand their food supply and transform their environment, worldwide population growth is not a problem. Overall, he contends, humans have never been as well fed as they are today. In fact, according to Eberstadt, food is growing less scarce and becoming less expensive. He maintains that affluence has changed patterns of economic activity around the world, resulting in a greater demand for services and a decrease in the world's use of natural resources. Nicholas Eberstadt is the Henry Wendt Scholar in Political Economy at the American Enterprise Institute for Public Policy Research.

As you read, consider the following questions:

1. According to Eberstadt, why do some people think there is a population problem?
2. What does Eberstadt say is responsible for the population explosion of the twentieth century?
3. How much has global gross domestic product increased since 1900, in Eberstadt's opinion?

The view that human beings are inexorably outstripping the globe's capacity to sustain them is one of the most vivid, powerful and enduring economic notions of the modern era. Since T.R. Malthus' 1798 treatise on population, the argument that the exponential growth of people and their demands will eventually exceed the earth's capacity has convinced successive generations of concerned scientists and laypersons that a serious "population problem" is imminent, and requires immediate action.

At first glance, this looks intuitively obvious. The planet, after all, is of a fixed size, and at some point will necessarily be unable to meet a continually rising demand upon its resources.

Human beings, however, are not like other animals. The Malthusian population-resource calculus does not consign our species to brutish subsistence, because our species, unlike all others, can consciously apply problem-solving techniques to the project of expanding its resource base and tempering its immediate environment.

Human beings can purposely transform their survival prospects, and they have done so dramatically, across the entire planet. Life expectancy today, for example, is over twice as high as a century ago. In the places conventionally deemed most prone to Malthusian calamity, moreover, improvements in longevity have been especially striking. During the past half-century, life expectancy in the less developed regions has jumped dramatically while the overall infant-mortality rate has significantly decreased. This "health explosion," not some improvident shift in procreation patterns, entirely accounts for the unprecedented "population explosion" of the 20th century.

Human Productivity Increases to Meet Demand

The same factors that have made our health revolution possible—advances in scientific and technological knowledge, the spread of education, improvements in organizational technique, and the like—have also supported a spectacular, and ongoing, increase in human productivity. Human beings, unlike any other living creatures, can progressively and intentionally augment the "resource base" that sustains them.

The point is illustrated vividly by the race between population and food over the course of the 20th century. Between 1900 and 2000, the world's population is thought to have nearly quadrupled. But this extraordinary population explosion did not consign humanity to mounting hunger. Just the opposite: Mankind enjoys a far better diet today than it did when the Earth's population was only one-fourth as large.

Overpopulation Is Not a Problem

A long-awaited world crisis of overpopulation is not developing. Indeed, declining population looms as a problem for many countries.

Finally, after all these years of demographic doomsaying, population proliferationism, and exponential extrapolated explosionism, comes a new report from the United Nations and a headline in the *New York Times*: "World Is Less Crowded Than Expected."

Ben J. Wattenberg, *AEI On the Issues*, December 1996.

Although millions live under the threat of deadly hunger, the inescapable fact of the matter is that humanity has never before been as well-fed as it is today, and that our improvements in nutritional well-being coincided with the most massive and rapid increase in population in the human experience. In fact, despite our species' exponentially increasing demand for food, there is compelling evidence that foodstuffs are actually growing ever less scarce: Real prices for corn, wheat and rice have plummeted by more than 70 percent since 1900.

A sophisticated neo-Malthusian may reason that food happens to be only one of the many resources upon which people depend and given its insatiable desire for improved consumption, mankind's appetite for resource use, which spirals upward even more rapidly than its population levels, must eventually come into disastrous collision against some limiting natural constraint.

The picture of the recent past, however, does not comport with the neo-Malthusian's proposed tableau of a world being steadily denuded of resources by unchecked population growth and consumerism. Paradoxically, despite humanity's burgeoning and indeed accelerating demand for consumption, global natural resource constraints over the past century have not obviously been tightening—and by some important indications, even appear to have been loosening. Since 1900, global gross domestic product, and thus global demand for goods and services, has increased almost 20-fold. Despite this staggering increase in demand, however, the relative price of primary commodities dropped markedly, an unfathomable and inexplicable result by Malthusian logic.

Looking toward the future, the Malthusian camp and its followers in the media imagine that human demands upon a fragile planet are poised to rise indefinitely. Yet even this assumption may be wrong. For one thing, patterns of economic activity around the globe have changed radically over the past century. With affluence, the shares in overall output of agriculture and manufacturing which draw heavily upon natural resources decrease progressively, and the share accounted for by services rises correspondingly.

Second, it is far from certain that the human population will be growing throughout the coming millennium, even if humanity were to enjoy all the benefits of orderly progress. In every industrial democracy in the contemporary world, fertility levels are below the replacement level in some of them, far below it. Sub-replacement fertility, moreover, is increasingly prevalent in low-income countries as well. If the pace of global fertility decline observed over the past 35 years were to continue for another quarter-century, human numbers would peak around the year 2040, and a world depopulation would commence thereafter.

None of this is to suggest that concern with humanity's current and prospective impact on the global environment is unwarranted. Quite the contrary. Strident and confident assertions by Malthusians and eco-activists notwithstanding, we understand all too little today about this extraordinarily complex dynamic. The case for conservation of, and stewardship over, natural resources would seem compelling but cannot be promoted by a worldview that strips mankind of its unique human dignity, any more than the Earth's "carrying capacity" for human beings can be established through rules and parameters derived from populations of fruit flies.

"Genetically modified (GM) crops, in combination with other technological innovations, will be a great help [in reducing world poverty]."

Genetically Modified Crops Are Helping to Reduce World Hunger

Willy De Greef

In the following viewpoint, Willy De Greef argues that the only options for reducing hunger are to farm more land or increase the yield of land currently under production. He maintains that because farming more land is ecologically unsound, increasing the yield of existing farmland using genetically modified (GM) crops offers the best solution to world hunger. GM crops, he asserts, will not only help poor farmers produce better, cheaper food, it will also help them generate income to lift themselves out of poverty. Willy De Greef is the head of regulatory and government affairs for Novartis Seeds AG in Switzerland.

As your read, consider the following questions:

1. According to De Greef, where will 90 percent of the world's population growth occur?
2. What farmer's resource is most scale-independent, in the author's opinion?
3. Who benefited most from the first GM crops grown, according to De Greef?

Willy De Greef, "Challenging the Food Crisis: Is There a Place for Biotechnology in Agriculture?" *OECD Observer*, Summer 2000, p. 84. Copyright © 2000 by *OECD Observer*. Reproduced by permission.

The world faces the extraordinary challenge of feeding perhaps nine billion people by the middle of the twenty-first century. The United Nations has been telling us for years, rightly, that it is a profound moral imperative to make a success of it. The big change in the past decade is that few people now doubt it can be done. The question now is: in what way? Can wise policy and clever technology combine to deliver a new and sustainable agriculture? Can poor countries develop the means of providing for themselves with dignity? We feel confident that seed development, including new methods of genetic modification, can and will play a big part in meeting these challenges.

The Food and Agriculture Organization of the United Nations (FAO) predicts that perhaps 90 percent of the massive world population growth will be in developing countries, and much of it in cities. In much of Asia and Latin America, food production has so far outpaced population growth, because yields have increased dramatically. But even there, and even more so in Africa, great increases will still be needed in yield and quality of food crops. Crucially, it is the amount, type and timing of all sorts of inputs which will determine whether the food is produced in an environmentally sound way—and that is true everywhere in the world.

Those with an informed understanding of agriculture have to remind the public of the value of the agricultural progress that has already been made. It also has to be stressed that it is possible to move forward innovation and the use of science and technology.

Just as boiling water can either make a nice cup of tea or scald, a biotechnology can be a powerful instrument for good, if it is directed at the right target. The target is the immense challenge presented by the World Food Summit to the agricultural community: essentially eradicate hunger in the next few decades, while making agriculture more sustainable. The production vs. distribution debate on the causes of continued undernourishment is a false debate. In the real world we need to vastly improve both. While distribution of food is clearly crucial to eradicating hunger, producing the food for distribution is an agricultural challenge of equally daunting proportions.

More Food Must Be Produced Without Using More Land

There are only two components to influence the supply side of food security: to produce more food, we can either increase the land under cultivation or increase yield on already cultivated land. That's it. Irrespective of improving distribution to the most needy, we only have those two options at the global level. In reality we only have one, since increasing land under cultivation is becoming increasingly untenable from an environmental viewpoint.

Last year the Subsidiary Body on Scientific, Technical and Technological Advice (SBSTTA) of the Biodiversity Convention (CBD) ranked habitat loss as the most important threat to global biodiversity. Much of this loss was due to the expansion of cultivated land. The challenge for biotechnology is to contribute to finding a solution to this threat by improving yield in a sustainable manner.

Management is the key to making this work while reducing the global footprint of agriculture on the environment. We see this with the Green Revolution of modern "conventional" seeds and chemicals. They have made the preservation of a viable wild and semi-wild habitat easier to achieve by allowing vast parts of the world to meet the population boom of the second half of the 20th century virtually without increasing the cultivated land area. They have already produced a better living for farmers with lower-impact inputs in much of Asia and Latin America. Conversely, FAO studies show that in Africa, where the Green Revolution has been slow to take off, increased food production is hard to achieve without putting more land under the plough.

Genetically modified (GM) crops, in combination with other technological innovations, will be a great help here. But to deliver on the promise of these technologies, it is essential to have an informed societal consensus, leading to realistic policies. Industry wants to take part in and promote such a debate, but cannot drive it alone. We believe that only an inclusive debate will ensure that rational rules and laws are in place for the development of biotechnology and its application will be adapted to rich and poor countries alike.

Biotechnology Is No Silver Bullet

Obviously, individual nations will legislate for the development of these new technologies according to their own needs and the expressed views of their citizens. Nonetheless, we believe that democratic legislation should take into account the powerful moral imperatives for viewing this technology with hope, not scepticism. We take great heart that independent voices such as the Nuffield Foundation's Council on Bioethics have framed this discussion. We agree with them, and with Professor Gordon Conway of the Rockefeller Foundation, that the benefits of biotechnology are not "silver bullets" or inevitably beneficial to all. But even a nuanced view accepts insights that many of the critics of biotechnology ignore.

The Poorest Farmers Could Be Helped by GM Crops

Hitherto, the success of the Green Revolution has depended on working to blueprints of desirable new plant and animal types through painstaking conventional plant breeding. Biotechnology, and especially genetic engineering, offers a faster route and also the means of tackling the particularly intractable problems of drought, salinity, and toxicity that typically face the poorest farmers on the marginal lands.

Gordon Conway, *Social Research*, Spring 1999.

Firstly, GM technologies will help farmers of many different sorts. The family farm everywhere—from the prairies of North America to the shambas of Africa—is under threat. But far from helping only big farmers, in North America GM seeds are already helping farmers of almost every scale to be more profitable. Quality seed is the farmer's resource that is most scale-independent in its beneficial effects. It is indeed because of this that the Green Revolution was able to lift so many millions of farmers out of poverty. The "Doubly Green Revolution", another vision of Conway, will integrate our lessons from mistakes of the past in reaching as many farmers as possible.

Naturally, the first crops grown with GM seeds were those that brought economic or other advantages to Western producers and consumers. Companies develop products for markets which can reward investment and business risk. In doing so, they are working in markets rich enough to support the enormous cost of the development and regulatory scrutiny needed for pioneering technologies. Now, however, we see developments in GM rice enhanced to provide vitamin A, and many other crops, including tropical subsistence crops, which will help farmers reduce costly and damaging inputs, whilst improving the nutritional quality of their produce. As Prof. Conway told the *Financial Times* recently: "There are about 1,000 Third World biotechnologists working on crop varieties, mostly rice. The debate is going on in the north and we're not hearing the voices coming from the developing world."

GM Crops Must Benefit the Poorest Farmers

Secondly, it is true that almost all technological developments have tended to pass by the very poorest farmers in the world. That sad fact is no reason to ignore the potential value of this technology to them. Getting GM technologies to the poorest farmers may need imaginative support schemes, perhaps along the lines being developed to bring drugs to the aid of poor sufferers of AIDS and malaria. The US Congress has just agreed to support work on GM crops in tropical agriculture research centres—a welcome reverse to a recent weakening or such international funding. Many countries will need help with building the right regulatory framework for these developments, as the Biosafety Protocol usefully encourages.

In the West, it is fashionable—but wrong—to divide the world into producers and consumers. In Africa, where 60 per cent of the consumers are the producers themselves, helping the farmers is the shortest route to helping the majority of the population. Africa and many other parts of the world are desperate for wealth-creating business. The equitable distribution of abundant food requires that the poor be sufficiently enriched to buy it. Biotechnology will help farmers in poor countries to generate not only cheaper and better food for local consumption, but also the incomes on which modern societies can be built.

As corporate citizens, we are keenly aware that we do most good when the social and legal framework is right. We are keen on rigorous, sensible regulation, since it ensures us "a licence to operate" while providing us with the trust of the society of which we are part. In the case of GM crops especially, we rely on international and national official support for the fundamental case underpinning progress, and for the regulatory framework which ensures it is safe, orderly and equitable.

"The genetic engineering revolution has nothing to do with feeding the world's hungry."

Genetically Modified Crops Are Not Reducing World Hunger

John Robbins

In the following viewpoint, John Robbins argues that genetically engineered (GE) crops are benefiting the companies that have patented the seeds and rich countries that use them to produce animal feed, not poor countries with hungry people to feed. He contends that if companies really wanted to help poor countries, they would instead develop GE crops that grow in marginal soil; produce high quality protein for humans without expensive machinery, fertilizers, or water; and favor small farms over large farms. John Robbins is the author of *Diet for a New America* and founder of Earth Save International.

As you read, consider the following questions:

1. According to Robbins, which three countries accounted for 99 percent of the world's genetically engineered plantings?
2. How does the yield of transgenic soybeans compare to that of conventional varieties, as reported by the author?
3. How did UN Food and Agriculture Organization delegates from Africa react to Monsanto's advertisements, as cited by Robbins?

John Robbins, "Are Genetically Altered Foods the Answer to World Hunger?" *Earth Island Journal*, vol. 16, Winter 2001, p. 26. Copyright © 2001 by John Robbins. Reproduced by permission of the author.

Biotechnology is one of tomorrow's tools in our hands today. Slowing its acceptance is a luxury our hungry world cannot afford.

—Monsanto advertisement

Genetically engineered crops were created not because they're productive but because they're patentable. Their economic value is oriented not toward helping subsistence farmers to feed themselves but toward feeding more livestock for the already overfed rich.

—Amory and Hunter Lovins,
Founders of the Rocky Mountain Institute

The global acreage planted in genetically engineered foods grew nearly 25-fold in the three years after 1996, the first year of large-scale commercialization. Yet this enormous growth took place almost entirely in only three countries.

In 1999, the United States by itself accounted for 72 percent of the crops. Argentina was responsible for another 17 percent and Canada weighed in with another 10 percent. These three countries together accounted for 99 percent of the entire planet's genetically engineered plantings.

Monsanto and other proponents of biotechnology continually tell the public that genetic engineering is necessary if the world's food supply is to keep up with population growth. But even with nearly 100 million acres planted, their products have yet to do a thing to reverse the spread of hunger. There is no more food available for the world's less fortunate. In fact, most of the fields were growing transgenic soybeans and corn that are destined for livestock feed.

Current GE Crops Will Not Solve Global Food Shortages

One of the clearest independent voices in the sometimes raucous debate about genetically modified foods is *Rachel's Environment and Health Weekly*. In 1999, the journal noted that "Neither Monsanto nor any of the other genetic engineering companies appears to be developing genetically engineered crops that might solve global food shortages." If genetically engineered crops were aimed at feeding the hungry, *Rachel's* noted, Monsanto would be developing seeds with certain predictable characteristics including:

- able to grow on substandard or marginal soils;
- able to produce more high-quality protein with increased per-acre yield, without the need for expensive machinery, chemicals, fertilizers or water;
- engineered to favor small farms over larger farms;
- cheap and freely available without restrictive licensing; and
- designed for crops that feed people, not meat animals.

"None of the genetically engineered crops now available, or in development (to the extent that these have been announced) has any of these desirable characteristics," *Rachel's* reports. "The genetic engineering revolution has nothing to do with feeding the world's hungry."

McMillan. © 2000 by Stephanie McMillan. Reprinted with permission.

If genetically engineered (GE) plants were designed to reverse world hunger, you would expect them to bring higher yields. But there is increasing evidence that they do just the opposite. Ed Oplinger, a professor of agronomy at the University of Wisconsin, has been conducting performance trials for soybean varieties for the past 25 years. In 1999, he compared the soybean yields in the 12 states that grew 80 percent of US soybeans and found that the yields from genetically modified soybeans were 4 percent lower than conventional varieties.

When other researchers compared the performance of Monsanto's transgenic soybeans (the world's number-one GE crop in terms of acreage planted) with those of conventional varieties grown under the same conditions, they found nearly a 10 percent yield reduction for the genetically engineered soybeans. And research done by the University of Nebraska in 2000 found the yields of GE soybeans were 6 to 11 percent lower than conventional plants.

Not that this research has hampered Dick Goddown, vice-president of the Biotechnology Industry Organization, from repeating the refrain that genetic engineering "is the best hope we have, as denizens of this planet, of being able to feed the people who are going to be on it."

African Delegates Reject Transgenic Technology

If genetically modified foods really were an answer to world hunger, it would be a powerful and persuasive argument in their favor. How could anyone stand in the way of feeding desperate and starving people? But Dr. Vandana Shiva, one of the world's foremost experts on world hunger and transgenic crops, claims that the argument that biotechnology will help feed the world "is on every level a deception . . . Soybeans go to feed the pigs and the cattle of the North. All the investments in agriculture are about increasing chemical sales and increasing monopoly control. All this is taking place in the private domain, by corporations that are not in the business of charity. They are in the business of selling. The food they will produce will be even more costly."

Similarly, delegates from 18 African countries at a meeting of the UN Food and Agriculture Organization responded to

Monsanto's advertisements with a clear statement: "We . . . strongly object that the image of the poor and hungry from our countries is being used by giant multinational corporations to push a technology that is neither safe, environmentally friendly, nor economically beneficial to us. We do not believe that such companies or gene technologies will help our farmers to produce the food that is needed . . . On the contrary . . . it will undermine our capacity to feed ourselves."

In 2000, a coalition of biotech companies began a $50 million media campaign to keep fears about genetically altered foods from spreading through the US. Bankrolling the campaign (which included $32 million in TV and print advertising) were Monsanto, Dow Chemical, DuPont, Swiss-based Novartis, the British Zeneca, Germany's BASF and Aventis of France. The ads, complete with soft-focus fields and smiling children, pitched "solutions that could improve our world tomorrow" and could help end world hunger.

Periodical Bibliography

The following articles have been selected to supplement the diverse views presented in this chapter.

African News Service	"Population Factors in Poverty Reduction," December 9, 2002.
Dennis Avery	"Feeding the World with Biotech Crops," *World & I*, May 1998.
Rommer M. Balaba	"Population Programs Key to Reducing Poverty—UN," *Asia Africa Intelligence Wire*, December 3, 2002.
Robert J. Borro	"The Myth That Poverty Breeds Terrorism," *BusinessWeek*, June 10, 2002.
Halle Dale	"Poverty and Terrorism," *Washington Times*, March 20, 2002.
Gill Donovan	"Vatican Denies Connection Between Poverty, Population," *National Catholic Reporter*, November 15, 2002.
Daniel T. Griswold	"The Blessings and Challenges of Globalization," *International Journal of World Peace*, September 2000.
Kathleen Hart	"Biotech Crops Pushed for Developing Nations," *Food Chemical News*, July 16, 2001.
Mark Hertsgaard	"A Global Green Deal: The Bad News Is That We Have to Change Our Ways—and Fast. Here's the Good News: It Could Be a Hugely Profitable Enterprise," *Time*, April 26, 2000.
Alan B. Krueger and Jitka Maleckova	"Does Poverty Cause Terrorism?" *New Republic Online*, June 24, 2002.
Kamal Mostafa Majumder	"Bangladesh: The Seeds of Change," *UNESCO Courier*, January 2001.
Linda Martin	"Six Billion and Counting," *Harvard International Review*, Fall 2000.
John Pilger	"The Real Story Behind America's War: John Pilger Reveals the Truth About How the Poor Nations Were Bled Dry by the Rich at the Last World Trade Conference in Doha," *New Statesman*, December 17, 2001.
Sarah Sexton and Nicholas Hildyard	"Genetic Engineering and World Hunger," *Synthesis/Regeneration*, Spring 1999.
Moin Siddiqi	"Poverty Is the Root of Terror," *African Business*, June 2002.
Kevin Watkins	"Making Globalization Work for the Poor," *Finance and Development*, March 2002.

For Further Discussion

Chapter 1

1. Food First regards hunger as a significant national problem that must be solved. It argues that freedom from hunger is a right. On the contrary, Robert Rector contends that hunger is a minimal, short-term problem for a very few people. Who makes the stronger argument? Why?

2. Dennis P. Andrulis contends that poor people who lack health insurance cannot access the health care they need and lead sicker, shorter lives. Tom Miller maintains that being poor and uninsured, alone, does not cause ill health. He argues that good health is primarily a result of education and a healthy lifestyle. Based on Andrulis's and Miller's viewpoints, which do you think would offer greater health improvements to the poor—insurance that provides easier access to health care or general education and training in healthy life choices?

3. The editors of *America* argue that homelessness in a prosperous United States is a disgrace and that compassion for the homeless demands that solutions to the problem be found. Leo K. O'Drudy III contends that identifying with the homeless will make Americans who have a place to live fearful of the future, doubtful of the justice of capitalism, and ashamed of the American way of life. Do you think the American way of life helps individuals prosper or does capitalism create a divided society between the "haves" and "have nots?" Explain.

Chapter 2

1. Isabel V. Sawhill focuses on out-of-wedlock births as a primary cause of poverty and maintains that unless unmarried women— particularly teens—stop having babies, they and their children are destined for a lifetime of poverty and welfare. Susan Douglas and Meredith Michaels argue that by depicting welfare mothers as lazy and dishonest, women's magazines have distorted America's perception of them. Douglas and Michaels maintain that most welfare mothers make the best decisions they can under difficult economic circumstances that are often beyond their control; they do not deserve to be blamed for all of society's ills. Which viewpoint do you think is most convincing? Why?

2. Robert Kaestner and Harold A. Pollack examine research into the link between substance abuse and poverty. Government pol-

icy is often determined by research of the type analysed in these viewpoints. Based on Kaestner's argument that drug abuse causes poverty, government policy should emphasize drug treatment to reduce poverty. However, based on Pollack's argument that factors other than drug abuse have a greater impact on poverty, government policy should emphasize education, help with transportation needs, and provide solutions to mental and physical health problems rather than offer drug treatment. Which viewpoint do you think is more likely to influence government policy? Why?

3. Joel Schwartz argues that poverty is caused by a failing of character—if poor people were thriftier and more diligent they would not be poor. Ellen Mutari insists that a lack of opportunities keep poor people from climbing out of poverty. That is, no matter how hardworking they are, people earning minimum wage cannot support themselves in most cities. Which viewpoint do you think portrays poverty more accurately? Please explain.

4. Gregory D. Squires argues that nearly a century of institutionalized prejudicial practices by mortgage lenders and property insurers have resulted in poverty and segregation in American cities. John Hood contends that it is the personal characteristics of loan applicants that explain virtually all racial or ethnic disparities. Which author is more persuasive? Why?

Chapter 3

1. Wendell Primus and Kathryn Porter argue that major government programs such as Social Security and the Earned Income tax credit help poor people immensely. J.D. Tuccille maintains that government programs are wasteful failures and that individuals and voluntary organizations could help the poor more effectively and less expensively. Do you think that voluntary organizations would run into the same bureaucratic problems the government faces if they tried to deal with all of the poor people in the country? Explain.

2. Holly Sklar contends that the minimum wage has not kept pace with inflation or worker productivity and must be raised. Thomas Sowell insists that if the minimum wage is raised, low-skilled people will not be able to find jobs at all because employers will hire only high-skilled workers worth the increased wage. Examine the evidence that both authors provide to support their arguments. Which author is more persuasive? Why?

3. According to the U.S. Department of Health and Human Services, welfare reform has been successful in reducing welfare

caseloads and decreasing the percentage of Americans living below the federal poverty level. Debra Watson argues that welfare reform has hurt the poor and that the safety net of social services is at its lowest level in years. Which argument do you think is stronger? Why?

4. The government should divert welfare money into programs that promote marriage because marriage helps people lift themselves out of poverty and raise healthier children, according to Wade F. Horn. Jeanne Winner argues that the marriage promotion program diverts money and attention away from the real economic problems that poor people, especially poor women, face and offers them no legitimate help. If the government offers economic incentives to young poor people to encourage them to marry, is it discriminating against poor people who choose to stay single? Why or why not?

Chapter 4

1. Strobe Talbott argues that the poor support terrorism because they feel victimized by the modern world. He maintains that the best weapon the United States has against terrorism is economic aid. Jane R. Eisner contends that terrorism is politically, not economically, motivated, and maintains that encouraging democracy in non-Western nations is the best way to help developing nations. Whose argument is more convincing? Why?

2. Ian Vásquez argues that globalization gives developing nations a chance to reenact at a much faster pace the dramatic economic advancements that Western countries enjoyed in the 1800s. He contends that their development will advance more quickly because they are following an established route rather than breaking new ground. Antonia Jubasz maintains that rapid globalization following a Western pattern has resulted in the neglect of the current needs of poor people in developing countries. If Jubasz is correct, can this neglect be justified in the hope that as the economy develops all will benefit, or is globalization just an excuse for the rich to dominate the poor? Please explain your answer, citing from the viewpoints.

3. The *Population Reports* editors list the specific negative effects of rapid population growth on the development of poor countries. Nicholas Eberstadt maintains that from a global perspective, population is not a problem because human beings (as a group) have always been able to expand their food supply. In your opinion, should the impact of population be assessed country by

country or is the total number of people on earth the only important statistic? Explain.

4. Willy De Greef argues that while genetically modified (GM) crops have not yet benefited poor countries, they certainly have the potential to do so if given a chance. John Robbins contends that GM technologies were specifically created to benefit rich countries at the expense of poor countries. In your opinion, what role should GM crops play in developing countries? Explain.

Organizations to Contact

The editors have compiled the following list of organizations concerned with the issues debated in this book. The descriptions are derived from materials provided by the organizations. All have publications or information available for interested readers. The list was compiled on the date of publication of the present volume; the information provided here may change. Be aware that many organizations take several weeks or longer to respond to inquiries, so allow as much time as possible.

The American Enterprise Institute for Public Policy Research (AEI)
1150 17th St. NW, Washington, DC 20036
(202) 862-5800 • fax: (202) 862-7178
e-mail: info@aei.org • website: www.aei.org
The institution is dedicated to preserving and strengthening the foundations of freedom—limited government, private enterprise, vital cultural and political institutions, and a strong foreign policy and national defense—through scholarly research, open debate, and publications. AEI research covers economics and trade; social welfare; government tax, spending, regulatory and legal policies; domestic politics; international affairs; defense and foreign policies. The institute publishes dozens of books and hundreds of articles and reports each year, and a policy magazine, the *American Enterprise*.

The Brookings Institution
1775 Massachusetts Ave. NW, Washington, DC 20036-2188
(202) 797-6000 • fax: (202) 797-6004
e-mail: brookinfo@brook.edu • website: www.brookings.edu
The institution is devoted to nonpartisan research, education, and publication in economics, government, foreign policy, and the social sciences. Its principal purposes are to aid in the development of sound public policies and to promote public understanding of issues of national importance. It publishes the quarterly journal the *Brookings Review*, which periodically includes articles on poverty, and numerous books, including *The Urban Underclass*.

Cato Institute
1000 Massachusetts Ave. NW, Washington, DC 20001-5403
(202) 842-0200 • fax: (202) 842-3490
e-mail: cato@cato.org • website: www.cato.org
The institute is a libertarian public policy research organization that advocates limited government. It has published a variety of lit-

erature concerning poverty in its quarterly *Cato Journal* and in its *Policy Analysis* series.

The Center for Law and Social Policy (CLASP)
1015 15th St. NW, Suite 400, Washington, DC 20005
(202) 906-8000 • fax: (202) 842-2885
website: www.clasp.org
The center is a national nonprofit organization that seeks to improve the economic conditions of low-income families with children. The center analyzes federal and state policies and practice in the areas of welfare reform and workforce development and produces materials designed to explain the meaning and implications of these policies and practices for federal, state, and local officials, community organizations, and service providers. CLASP produces numerous individual publications on issues related to family economic security and civil legal assistance. All of these publications are free and can be downloaded from the center's website.

Center of Concern
3700 13th St. NE, Washington, DC 20017
(202) 635-2757 • fax: (202) 832-9494
e-mail: coc@igc.apc.org • website: www.coc.org/coc/
Center of Concern engages in social analysis, theological reflection, policy advocacy, and public education on issues of justice and peace. Its programs and writings include subjects such as international development, women's roles, economic alternatives, and a theology based on justice for all peoples. It publishes the bimonthly newsletter *Center Focus* as well as numerous papers and books, including *Opting for the Poor: A Challenge for North Americans.*

Center on Budget and Policy Priorities
820 1st St. NE, Suite 510, Washington, DC 20002
(202) 408-1080 • fax: (202) 408-1056
e-mail: center@center.cbpp.org • website: www.cbpp.org
The center promotes better public understanding of the impact of federal and state governmental spending policies and programs primarily affecting low- and moderate-income Americans. It acts as a research center and information clearinghouse for the media, national and local organizations, and individuals. The center publishes numerous fact sheets, articles, and reports, including *The Safety Net Delivers: The Effects of Government Benefit Programs in Reducing Poverty.*

Children's Defense Fund (CDF)

25 E St. NW, Washington, DC 20001
(202) 628-8787
e-mail: cdfinfo@childrensdefense.org
website: www.childrensdefense.org

CDF works to promote the interests of children in America. It pays particular attention to the needs of poor, minority, and disabled children. Its publications include *The State of America's Children 1998* and *Wasting America's Future: The Children's Defense Fund's Report on the Costs of Child Poverty*.

Coalition on Human Needs

1000 Wisconsin Ave. NW, Washington, DC 20007
(202) 342-0726 • fax: (202) 338-1856
e-mail: chn@chn.org

The coalition is a federal advocacy organization that works in such areas as federal budget and tax policy, housing, education, health care, and public assistance. It lobbies for adequate federal funding for welfare, Medicaid, and other social services. Its publications include *How the Poor Would Remedy Poverty*, the *Directory of National Human Needs Organizations*, and the biweekly legislative newsletter the *Human Needs Report*.

Economic Policy Institute (EPI)

1660 L St. NW, Suite 1200, Washington, DC 20036
(202) 775-8810 • (800) 374-4844 (publications)
(202) 331-5510 (Washington, DC)
e-mail: blustig@epinet.org • website: www.epinet.org

The institute was established in 1986 to pursue research and public education to help define a new economic strategy for the United States. Its goal is to identify policies that can provide prosperous, fair, and balanced economic growth. It publishes numerous policy studies, briefing papers, and books, including *State of Working America* and *Declining American Incomes and Living Standards*.

The Heritage Foundation

214 Massachusetts Ave. NE, Washington, DC 20002-4999
(202) 546-4400 • fax: (202) 546-8328
e-mail: info@heritage.org • website: www.heritage.org

The foundation is a public policy research institute dedicated to the principles of free competitive enterprise, limited government, individual liberty, and a strong national defense. The foundation publishes the monthly newsletter *Insider* and *Heritage Today*, a newsletter published six times per year, as well as various reports and journals.

Institute for Food and Development Policy
398 60th St., Oakland, CA 94618
(510) 654-4400 • fax: (510) 654-4551
e-mail: foodfirst@igc.apc.org • website: www.foodfirst.org

The institute is a research, documentation, and public education center focusing on the social and economic causes of world hunger. It believes that there is enough food in the world to adequately feed everyone, but hunger results "when people lack control over the resources they need to produce food." It publishes the quarterly *Food First Backgrounders* as well as numerous articles, pamphlets, and books, including *An Update of World Hunger: Twelve Myths*.

Institute for Research on Poverty (IRP)
University of Wisconsin-Madison
1180 Observatory Drive, 3412 Social Science Building
Madison, WI 53706-1393
(608) 262-6358 • fax: (608) 265-3119
e-mail: evanson@ssc.wisc.edu • website: www.ssc.wise.edu/irp

The Institute for Research on Poverty (IRP) is a national, university-based center for research into the causes and consequences of poverty and social inequality in the United States. It is nonprofit and nonpartisan. The principal activities of the institute are sponsorship of the original research of its members and dissemination of their findings. Seminars, workshops, conferences, and a publications program that includes print and electronic dissemination are designed to achieve those ends. The institute newsletter, *Focus*, discussion papers, and special reports are available online.

National Alliance to End Homelessness
1518 K St. NW, Suite 206, Washington, DC 20005
(202) 638-1526 • fax: (202) 638-4664
e-mail: naeh@naeh.org • website: www.naeh.org

The alliance is a national organization committed to the ideal that no American should have to be homeless. It works to secure more effective national and local policies to aid the homeless. Its publications include *What You Can Do to Help the Homeless* and the monthly newsletter *Alliance*.

National Center for Children in Poverty (NCCP)
Mailman School of Public Health, Columbia University
154 Haven Ave., New York, NY 10032
(212) 304-7100 • fax: (212) 544-4200
e-mail: nccp@columbia.edu • website: www.nccp.org

The center identifies and promotes strategies that prevent child poverty in the United States and that improve the lives of low-income children and their families. NCCP's social science research unit conducts original research and publishes reports that alert the nation to the threat posed by child poverty and gives policymakers insights into the dynamics of child poverty. In addition, the center publishes numerous reports, fact sheets, and opinion pieces, and uses online communications and library-based resources to disseminate a broad array of research-based information that is directly relevant to improving children's lives. The center commissions opinion research to gain a deeper understanding of public attitudes about child poverty and to gain insights into the attitudinal barriers that have prevented action to reduce child poverty.

National Council of La Raza (NCLR)
1111 19th St. NW, Suite 1000, Washington, DC 20036
(202) 785-1670 • fax: (202) 785-0851
e-mail: akadis@nclr.org • website: www.nclr.org

NCLR is a national organization that promotes civil rights and economic opportunities for Hispanics. It provides technical assistance to Hispanic organizations engaged in community development, including economic development, housing, employment and training, business assistance, health, and other fields. NCLR publishes a quarterly newsletter, *Agenda*, as well as other issue-specific newsletters on poverty.

National Student Campaign Against Hunger and Homelessness (NSCAHH)
11965 Venice Blvd., Suite 408, Los Angeles, CA 90066
(800) 664-8647 • (310) 397-5270 ext. 323 • fax: (310) 391-0053
e-mail: nscah@aol.com • website: www.nscahh.org

NSCAHH is a network of college and high school students, educators, and community leaders who work to fight hunger and homelessness in the United States and around the world. Its mission is to create a generation of student/community activists who will explore and understand the root causes of poverty and who will initiate positive change through service and action. It publishes the quarterly newsletter *Students Making a Difference* as well as numerous manuals, fact sheets, and handbooks.

Population Reference Bureau, Inc. (PRB)
1875 Connecticut Ave. NW, Suite 520
Washington, DC 20009-5728
(202) 483-1100 • fax: (202) 328-3937
e-mail: popref@prb.org • website: www.prb.org/prb

PRB gathers, interprets, and disseminates information on national and world population trends. Its publications include the quarterly *Population Bulletin* and the monthly *Population Today.*

Poverty and Race Research Action Council (PRRAC)
1711 Connecticut Ave. NW, # 207, Washington, DC 20009
(202) 387-9887 • fax: (202) 387-0764
e-mail: prrac@aol.com • website: www.prrac.org

PRRAC was established by civil rights, antipoverty, and legal services groups. It works to develop antiracism and antipoverty strategies and provides funding for research projects that support advocacy work. It publishes the bimonthly newsletter *Poverty & Race.*

Progressive Policy Institute (PPI)
316 Pennsylvania Ave. SE, Suite 555, Washington, DC 20003
(202) 547-0001
e-mail: webmaster@dlcppi.org • website: www.ndol.org

PPI develops policy alternatives to the conventional liberal-conservative political debate. It advocates social policies that move beyond merely maintaining the poor to liberating them from poverty and dependency. Its publications include *Microenterprise: Human Reconstruction in America's Inner Cities* and *Social Service Vouchers: Bringing Choice and Competition to Social Services.*

Urban Institute
2100 M St. NW, Washington, DC 20037
(202) 833-7200
e-mail: paffairs@ui.urban.org • website: www.urban.org

The Urban Institute investigates social and economic problems confronting the nation and analyzes efforts to solve these problems. In addition, the institute works to improve government decisions and their implementation and to increase citizen awareness about important policy decisions. It offers a wide variety of resources, including books such as *Restructuring Medicare: Impacts on Beneficiaries* and *The Decline in Medical Spending Growth in 1996: Why Did It Happen?*

The Welfare Information Network (WIN)

1401 New York Ave. NW, Suite 800, Washington, DC 20005
(202) 587-1000 • fax: (202) 628-4205
e-mail: bvlare@financeproject.org
website: www.financeprojectinfo.org

A project of The Finance Project, WIN is a clearinghouse for information, policy analysis, and technical assistance related to welfare, workforce development, and other human and community services. The Finance Project is a nonprofit policy research, technical assistance, and information organization created to help improve outcomes for children, families, and communities nationwide. Its mission is to support decision making that produces and sustains good results by developing and disseminating information, knowledge, tools, and technical assistance for improved policies, programs, and financing strategies. It produces a broad array of publications and information resources. Most are available online.

Bibliography of Books

Randy Albelda and Ann Withorn, eds.	*Lost Ground: Welfare Reform, Poverty, and Beyond.* Cambridge, MA: South End Press, 2002.
Dwight B. Billings and Kathleen M. Blee	*The Road to Poverty: The Making of Wealth and Hardship in Appalachia.* New York: Cambridge University Press, 2000.
Douglas H. Boucher and Douglas M. Boucher, eds.	*The Paradox of Plenty: Hunger in a Bountiful World.* Oakland, CA: First Food Press, 1999.
Martha Burt et al.	*Helping America's Homeless: Emergency Shelter or Affordable Housing.* Washington, DC: Urban Institute Press, 2001.
John Cavanagh et al.	*Alternatives to Economic Globalization.* San Francisco: Berrett-Koehler, 2002.
Ram A. Cnaan et al.	*The Invisible Caring Hand: American Congregations and the Provision of Welfare.* New York: New York University Press, 2002.
Chuck Collins and Felice Yeskel	*Economic Apartheid in America: A Primer on Economic Inequality and Security.* New York: New Press, 2000.
Dalton Conley	*Being Black, Living in the Red: Race, Wealth, and Social Policy in America.* Berkeley, CA: University of California Press, 1999.
Dalton Conley, ed.	*Wealth and Poverty in America: A Reader.* Malden, MA: Blackwell, 2002.
Deborah R. Connolly	*Homeless Mothers: Face to Face with Women and Poverty.* Minneapolis: University of Minnesota Press, 2002.
Sheldon Danziger and Ann Chih Lin, eds.	*Coping with Poverty: The Social Contexts of Neighborhood, Work, and Family in the African-American Community.* Ann Arbor: University of Michigan Press, 2000.
Sheldon Danziger and Robert H. Haveman, eds.	*Poverty.* Cambridge, MA: Harvard University Press, 2002.
Laurie Fields Derose et al.	*Who's Hungry and How Do We Know? Food Shortage, Poverty, and Deprivation.* New York: United Nations University Press, 1999.
Barbara Ehrenreich	*Nickel and Dimed: On (Not) Getting By in America.* New York: Henry Holt, 2002.

D. Stanley Eitzen et al.	*Experiencing Poverty: Voices from the Bottom.* Belmont, CA: Wadsworth, 2002.
Ross Fergusson and Gordon Hughes, eds.	*Ordering Lives: Family, Work, and Welfare.* New York: Routledge, 2000.
Lynnell Hancock	*Hands to Work: The Stories of Three Families Racing the Welfare Clock.* New York: William Morrow, 2001.
Sharon Hays	*Flat Broke with Children: Women in the Age of Welfare Reform.* New York: Oxford University Press, 2003.
Susan Holloway et al.	*Through My Own Eyes: Single Mothers and the Cultures of Poverty.* Cambridge, MA: Harvard University Press, 2001.
Charles W. Kegley Jr., ed.	*The New Global Terrorism: Characteristics, Causes, Controls.* Upper Saddle River, NJ: Prentice-Hall, 2002.
Frances Moore Lappe et al.	*World Hunger: Twelve Myths.* New York: Grove Press, 1998.
George S. McGovern	*The Third Freedom: Ending Hunger in Our Time.* New York: Rowman and Littlefield, 2002.
Gwendolyn Mink	*Welfare's End.* Ithaca, NY: Cornell University Press, 2002.
Deepa Narayan and Patti Petesch, eds.	*Voices of the Poor: From Many Lands.* Washington, DC: Oxford University Press and the World Bank, 2002.
David Neumark	*How Living Wage Laws Affect Low-Wage Workers and Low-Income Families.* San Francisco: Public Policy Institute of California, 2002.
Katherine S. Newman	*No Shame in My Game: The Working Poor in the Inner City.* New York: Vintage Books, 2000.
James T. Patterson	*America's Struggle Against Poverty in the Twentieth Century.* Cambridge, MA: Harvard University Press, 2000.
Per Pinstrup-Andersen and Ebbe Schioler	*Seeds of Contention: World Hunger and the Global Controversy over GM (Genetically Modified) Crops.* Washington, DC: International Food Policy Research Institute, 2001.
Bradley R. Schiller	*The Economics of Poverty and Discrimination,* 8th ed. Upper Saddle River, NJ: Prentice-Hall, 2001.
Loretta Schwartz-Nobel	*Growing Up Empty: The Hunger Epidemic in America.* New York: HarperCollins, 2002.

213

Holly Sklar et al.   *Raise the Floor: Wages and Policies That Work for Us All.* New York: Ms. Foundation for Women, 2001.

Joseph E. Stiglitz   *Globalization and Its Discontents.* New York: W.W. Norton, 2002.

Jerold L. Waldman   *The Politics of the Minimum Wage.* Urbana: University of Illinois Press, 2000.

Index

abortion, 62
Adler, Nancy, 39
Africa, 13, 14, 183, 192–93
  impact of AIDS in, 156–57
  need for increased crop yields in,
    190
  terrorism not a serious problem in,
    166
African Americans, 20, 22, 61, 151
  decline of single motherhood and,
    63
  media stereotyping of, 65, 69, 70
  obesity and, 26
  reduction in poverty and, 136, 137
  see also discrimination
AIDS, 34–35, 63, 193
  HIV Outcomes Study and, 32–33
  impact of, on poor countries,
    156–57
AIDS Epidemic Update 2002
  (UNAIDS and WHO), 157
Aid to Families with Dependent
  Children (AFDC), 83, 135
Akerlof, George, 62–63
Albelda, Randy, 70
Alexander, Rachel, 124
Al-Sultan, Fawzi H., 14
America (periodical), 47
American Economic Review
  (periodical), 97
American Enterprise Institute for
  Public Policy Research, 83, 185
American Family Mutual Insurance
  Company, 100
American Journal of Public Health, 80
Andrulis, Dennis P., 28
Arab region, 162, 165, 166
Argentina, 171, 196
Arizona Daily Wildcat (newspaper),
  124
Asia, 13, 14, 169, 177, 183
  effect of genetically modified crops
    in, 190, 191
Aslund, Anders, 170
Atlanta, 49
Attanasio, Orazio, 42

Barone, Michael, 86
Barro, Robert, 172
Bauer, Peter, 133
Bayh, Evan, 149
Becker, Gary, 106

Bennett, William, 67
bin Laden, Osama, 159–60
Biodiversity Convention (CBD), 191
Biosafety Protocol, 193
Biotechnology Industry
  Organization, 198
Black Enterprise (periodical), 107
Bloch, Howard R., 108
Bloom, Allan, 67
Bost, Eric M., 18
Boston, 48, 93
Boston Globe (newspaper), 71–72
British Retirement Survey, 42
Brookings Institution, 59
Brooks, Jennifer, 89–90, 92
Brown, Murphy, 67
Bush, George H.W., 52, 69, 159
Bush, George W., 52, 127, 163, 175,
  176
  administration's attitude to
    marriage and, 143, 148, 149
  TANF program reauthorized by,
    134, 135
business
  benefits of GM crops for, 192–93,
    195, 198–99
  minimum wages and, 128–29
  women and minority owners in,
    105, 106–107
  see also globalization

Canada, 31, 196
Caplan, Arthur, 36
*Care Without Coverage: Too Little, Too
  Late* (Institute of Medicine), 38
Carter, Stephen, 105
Casanova, C., 31
Casse, Daniel, 87
Cato Institute, 37, 123, 167, 168
caucasians, 20, 22
Causes of Vulnerability, The (Haas and
  Adler), 39
Census Bureau, U.S., 12, 118, 136,
  139
  data on poverty and, 117, 140
Center for Studying Health Systems
  Change, 30
Center on Budget and Policy
  Priorities (CBPP), 116–21, 139,
  140, 141
Centers for Disease Control and
  Prevention, 34, 35

Central African Republic, 157
charity, 87, 122, 145
  success of, in addressing poverty,
    124–25
Chicago, 49, 93
child care, 62, 83, 89, 127, 128
children, 114, 115, 156–57
  effect of poor health care
    provisions on, 29–30, 33
  impact of government benefits on,
    116
    includes reduction in poverty,
      119, 136–37
      con, 138–41
    weakening effects of, 117,
      120–21
  homelessness and, 48
  hunger among, 20–22
    is minimal, 25
  illegitimacy and, 27, 59–61
  obesity and, 26
  promotion of marriage important
    for, 143–44
    con, 148–51
child support laws, 64
China, 14, 170
CIA (Central Intelligence Agency),
  176, 177
Clinton, Bill, 52, 69, 119, 149
  administration's welfare reform
    and, 139–41
Community Reinvestment Act
  (CRA), 97, 98, 99, 102
Conference on Women in the War
  on Poverty, 12
Congress, U.S., 36, 89, 149, 176,
  193
  authority of president to sidestep,
    179
  housing equity and, 97, 99, 102
  war on terrorism and, 158, 161
  welfare reform policy and, 139,
    141
contraception, 62, 63, 181
Conway, Gordon, 192, 193
Council on Bioethics (Nuffield
  Foundation), 192

Dallas, 50
De Greef, Willy, 189
democracy, 163–66, 188, 192
  need to promote, 160
Denver, 48
De Parle, Jason, 71, 85
Department of Agriculture, U.S.

(USDA), 17–18, 20, 26–27, 90
Department of Health and Human
  Services, U.S. (HHS), 25, 114,
  134, 135, 142, 180
Department of Housing and Urban
  Development (HUD), 50, 97–98,
  101
Department of Justice (DOJ), 97,
  98, 101
DiLorenzo, Thomas J., 26
discrimination
  against African Americans and
    Latinos regarding housing,
    95–100
  exaggerations about, 104, 109
  institutional, 101
  need for Congress to address,
    102
  need to educate consumers to
    prevent, 103
  poverty perpetuated by, 94, 98
  competition can eliminate, 106,
    110
  reduction in, 105
    in employment, 107–108
divorce, 59, 60, 150
Dollars and Sense (periodical), 70,
  148
Douglas, Susan, 65

Earned Income Tax Credit (EITC),
  64, 116–21, 128, 141
Eberstadt, Nicholas, 185
*Economic Expansions Are Unhealthy:
  Evidence from Microdata* (Ruhm),
  44
Economic Freedom of the World (Fraser
  Institute), 168
Economist (periodical), 178–79
economy, 85, 129, 161, 184
  global changes in, 188
  gross domestic product (GDP)
    and, 178, 182, 183, 185, 188
  improvements in, 59, 64
    economic freedom a condition
      for, 168–70
    health benefits not guaranteed
      by, 44–45
    reduced poverty rates not
      guaranteed by, 20, 121, 152
    rule of law necessary for, 172–73
    welfare participation not
      determined by, 60
  see also globalization
education, 76, 87, 108, 114, 151

earning prospects and, 62
effect of, on land use, 14
health and, 41, 44, 46
housing and, 103
low quality of, in rural United
States, 12
marriage skills and, 142, 146
role of, in poverty prevention, 59,
150, 186
slow population growth a benefit
for, 181
substance abuse and, 81
teen mothers and, 61
terrorists not deterred by, 163–65
Eisner, Jane R., 162
elderly population, 20, 22, 30, 41–42
Social Security effective for,
117–18
emergency departments, 31
emergency food assistance, 21–22,
48, 50
Emmerson, Carl, 42
employment, 139
drug use and, 74, 81
emphasis on, in welfare reform,
85–86
low paid, 62, 71, 148, 151
population growth and, 181–82
poverty not prevented by, 89–93
reduction in earning potential for
unskilled men and, 61
reduction of discrimination in,
105–108
"Endangered Family, The,"
(Newsweek), 69
environment, 184, 191
Equal Credit Opportunity Act
(1974), 96–97
Europe, 168, 170–71
Exploring the Health-Wealth Nexus
(Meer, Rosen, and Douglas
Miller), 42

Fair Housing Act (1968), 96–97, 102
families, 85, 114–15
composition of, linked to poverty,
75–76
drug use and, 74
health care and, 57
homelessness and, 48
low income, 30, 88–93, 119–20,
127
subsidies needed for, 128
see also marriage; single
motherhood

Federal Housing Administration
(FHA), 95
Federal Reserve Bank of Boston, 97,
109
Ferara, Peter S., 123
fertility, decline in, 188
Fighting Poverty with Virtue
(Schwartz), 86
Financial Times (newspaper), 193
Fisher, Elliott, 42
food, 183
costs of, 90–91
hunger not prevented by mere
production of, 19–20, 190
improved availability of, 185, 187
need to produce sustainably, 191
see also Food Stamp program;
genetically modified (GM) crops
Food and Agriculture Organization
(FAO). See United Nations
Food First, 19
Food Stamp Act (1964), 17
Food Stamp Program, 18, 118, 120,
138, 140
hunger caused by changes in, 22
introduction of, 17
foreign aid, 160, 164, 173, 175, 177
48 Hours (CBS TV documentary),
70–71
Franks, P., 33
Fraser Institute, 168–72
Free-Market.Net Spotlight, 122
Free Trade Area of the Americas,
179
Friedman, Milton, 107

Gaston, A.B., 107
General Accounting Office report,
85
genetically engineered (GE) crops.
See genetically modified (GM)
crops
genetically modified (GM) crops
hunger can be reduced by, 189–93
con, 195–99
need for regulation of, 194
Germany, 31
Glass-Steagall Act, 99
globalization, 173
income gap increased by, 178
need for regulation of, 171–72, 174
wealthy people benefit from, 179
world poverty alleviated by,
167–70
con, 175–77

Goddown, Dick, 198
Goldman, Dana, 42–44
Good Housekeeping (magazine), 66
Goodman, John C., 123
government programs to address
poverty, 21, 113–14, 152
are effective, 116–19
con, 120–24
see also welfare participation;
welfare reform
Great Depression, 53, 139
Green Revolution, 191, 192
Greenspan, Alan, 99

Haas, Jennifer, 39
Hadley, Jack, 33, 39–40
Hale, Roslyn, 71
Head Start project, 147
criticisms of, 115
origin of, 114
Health Affairs (Wennberg, Fisher,
and Skinner), 41–42
health care, 12, 92, 127, 128
hospital services and, 30, 57
population growth and, 181
poverty affects access to, 90
need for action to reduce
disparities and, 29, 36
through lack of education, 43–44
through lack of health insurance,
28–33
con, 37–38, 42–43, 45–46
poverty affects quality of, 34–35
studies of, 39–41
women have less access to, 14
health problems, 25–26, 158, 193
mental, 48–49, 52, 54
single-parent families and, 61
see also AIDS; health care
Herger, Wally, 136
Heritage Foundation, 123
Hezbollah, 164
HIV. *See* AIDS
Hobbes, Thomas, 67
homelessness, 13, 85, 151
causes of, 48–50
is a serious problem for American
poor, 47
con, 51–54
Home Mortgage Disclosure Act
(HMDA), 97, 100, 101
Hood, John, 104
Hoover Institution, 130
Horn, Wade F., 142, 149
Hortobagyi, Paul, 132

housing, 13, 89–90, 145
assistance for low-income families
and, 118
lack of affordability and, 48
public, 50, 53, 87
urban vs. suburban, 96
see also discrimination
Housing Opportunities Made Equal
(HOME), 101
Hoyt, Homer, 94, 95
Hudson Institute, 108
Humane Studies Review (periodical),
125
human rights, 22–23, 178
hunger, 12, 17, 48, 158, 187
agriculture and, 191–92
famine and, 157
GM crops can reduce worldwide,
189, 193–94
con, 195–99
is a serious problem in U.S.,
18–23, 50, 151
con, 24–27
is a serious problem worldwide,
157, 183, 190
con, 185, 187
production and distribution of
food can reduce worldwide, 190

illiteracy, 14
India, 13–14, 170
Individual Development Accounts
(IDAs), 82, 84–85
Indonesia, 175, 177
infant
health, 28, 33, 41
mortality, 170, 186
Institute of Medicine (IOM), 29, 38
In Style (magazine), 67
*Insurance and the Utilization of
Medical Services Among the Self-
Employed* (Rosen and Perry), 45
International Fund for Agricultural
Development (IFAD), 14
International Monetary Fund (IMF),
173, 177–78

John Locke Foundation, 104
Johnson, Lyndon B., 114
Joint Center for Poverty Research, 78
Joint United Nations Program on
HIV/AIDS (UNAIDS), 156–57
Jubasz, Antonia, 175

Kaestner, Robert, 73

Kennedy, John F., 17
Kenya, 157
Kim, Marlene, 86
Koop, C. Everett, 26
Krueger, Alan B., 163–65

Lakdawalla, Darius, 43–44
Lal, Deepak, 173
Latin America, 13, 190, 191
Latinos, 20, 22
  obesity among, 26
  reduction in poverty among, 137
  see also discrimination
Laudan, Larry, 32
Lebanon, 164
Leef, George C., 107
Levy, Helen, 45–46
Libertarian Alliance, 125
life expectancy, 33, 186
literacy, 170
Lleras-Muney, Adriana, 44
Losing Ground (Murray), 123
Lovins, Amory and Hunter, 196

MacDonald, Heather, 53
Maleckova, Jitka, 164
Malthus, T.R., 186
  ideas of, 187–88
managed care, 36
marriage, 61–62
  drug use and, 76, 77
  government should promote,
    142–43, 147
    con, 148–50
  through premarital education,
    146
  through removing disincentives,
    145
  through teaching conflict
    management skills, 144
Mayne, Ed, 128
Mbeki, Thabo, 179
Meara, Ellen, 40–41
media, 65, 109
  stereotypes in, 67
    concerning welfare mothers,
      68–69, 71–72
    racial, 66, 70
Medicaid, 32, 33, 35, 41, 57
  tendency for poor health outcomes
    under, 40
Medical Outcomes Study, 33
Medicare, 30, 41–42
Meer, Jonathan, 42
Meltzer, David, 45–46

Mexico, 171
Michaels, Meredith, 65
Michigan Women's Employment
  Study (WES), 80
Micklethwait, Brian, 125
Micklethwait, John, 174
Miller, Douglas, 42
Miller, Tom, 37
minimum wage, 62, 126, 152
  earners of, are mostly young, 131
  history of, 127
  increase of, is needed, 91–92,
    128–29
    con, 130–32
  Third World suffering caused by,
    133
Monsanto company, 195–99
mortality, rates of, 38, 40, 44
motherhood, single. See single
  motherhood
Murray, Charles, 123
Mutari, Ellen, 88

NAACP v. American Family Mutual
  Insurance Company, 100
National Academy of Sciences, 118
National Association of Insurance
  Commissioners, 100
National Association of Realtors, 95
National Campaign to Prevent Teen
  Pregnancy, 59
National Center for Health
  Statistics, 30
National Center for Policy Analysis
  (NCPA), 123
National Coalition for the
  Homeless, 50
National Community Reinvestment
  Coalition, 99
National Fair Housing Alliance, 100
National Hospital Discharge Survey,
  30
National Household Survey of Drug
  Abuse (NHSDA), 75, 77, 79–80
National Law Center Study on
  Homelessness and Poverty in
  Washington, D.C., 47, 49–50
National Longitudinal Survey of
  Youth (NLSY), 75
National Medical Care Utilization
  and Expenditure Survey, 30
National Medical Expenditures
  Survey, 32
National Survey of America's
  Families, 145

Nationwide Insurance Company,
100–101
Newsweek (magazine), 43, 66, 69
New York City, 49, 53, 89, 91, 124
study on health care in, 34
New York Times (newspaper), 71, 85,
151, 187
1999 Human Development Report
(United Nations), 177
North American Free Trade
Agreement, 178
Nuffield Foundation, 192

obesity, 25, 44
among poor children, 26
O'Drudy, Leo K., III, 51
Office of Child Development in the
U.S., 114
Office of Economic Opportunity,
114
Ooms, Theodora, 151
Oplinger, Ed, 198
Organization of Economic
Development and Cooperation, 33
Orshansky, Mollie, 90–91

Pakistan, 175, 177
Pearce, Diana, 89–90, 92
People (magazine), 66
Perry, Craig, 45
Personal Responsibility and Work
Opportunity Reconciliation Act of
1997, 89, 139
Philadelphia, 48, 93
Philadelphia Inquirer (newspaper),
162
Philanthropy (magazine), 82, 85
Piot, Peter, 157
Pollack, Harold, 79
population growth
food supply and, 190, 196
minimal, in rural U.S., 13
world poverty exacerbated by,
180–84
con, 185–88
Population Reports (periodical), 180
Porter, Kathryn, 116, 139
poverty, 12–14
efforts to address, 14, 21, 59
encouragement of savings and,
84
importance of welfare subsidies
and, 92–93, 128
importance of work and, 85, 134,
136, 137

need to encourage value of
diligence and, 86–87
self-reliance a key to, 82
lack of earning potential a cause of,
88–93
lack of individual responsibility a
cause of, 82–83
method of assessing in U.S., 88,
90–91
prenatal programs, 41
Primus, Wendell, 116, 139, 140
Project on Global Economic
Liberty, 167

*Rachel's Environment and Health
Weekly* (journal), 196–97
racism, 95
Radu, Michael, 165
Rage over Welfare (TV program),
70–71
Raines, Franklin D., 98
*Raise the Floor: Wages and Policies
That Work for Us All* (Sklar), 126
RAND corporation, 43
Ransom, David, 160
Reader's Digest (magazine), 71
Reagan, Ronald, 52, 67, 69, 119, 152
*Recent Changes in the Impact of the
Safety Net on Child Poverty* (1999
report), 139
Rector, Robert, 24, 124
Reed, Gerald W., 123
*Relationship Between Education and
Adult Mortality in the United States*
(Lleras-Muney), 44
Riley, Tom, 85
Robbins, John, 195
Rogers, Beatrice, 17
Röpke, Wilhelm, 173
Rosen, Harvey, 42, 45
Ruhm, Christopher, 44
Russia, 171

Samuelson, Robert J., 43
San Francisco, 49
savings, 82–85, 180–83
Sawhill, Isabel V., 58
Schwartz, Joel, 82, 86
Second Harvest, 21, 25
Section 8 certificates, 50
self-employment, 45
*Self-Sufficiency Standard for the City
of New York, The* (Pearce and
Brooks), 88–92
Senate, U.S., 23, 123

September 11, 2001, terrorist attacks, 159–60, 176
Seventh Circuit Court of Appeals, 99
Shelley v. Kraemer, 95
shelters, homeless, 13, 48, 50
  increased need for, 47
Sherraden, Michael, 84
Shiva, Vandana, 177
Sicker and Poorer: The Consequences of Being Uninsured (Hadley), 39–40
Siddeley, Leslie, 125
single motherhood, 20, 74, 144, 149, 150
  decreasing rates of, 63
  increasing rates of, 60, 62
  media stereotypes concerning, 65, 72
    demonization of welfare mothers and, 69–71
    portrayal of celebrity mothers and, 66–68
  poverty caused by, 58–59, 64
  tendency of, to begin during teen years, 61
Sirico, Robert A., 125
Skinner, Jonathan, 42
Sklar, Holly, 126
Social Security, 117–18, 121
Social Security Administration, 90
Soto, Hernando de, 172
Sowell, Thomas, 130
Springfield, Jim, 17
Squires, Gregory D., 94
Starfield, B., 31
Strengths of the Safety Net (Center on Budget and Policy Priorities), 117
Styer, Tim, 129
Subsidiary Body on Scientific, Technical, and Technological Advice (SBSTTA), 191
substance abuse, 48, 52, 53, 85
  crime and, 27
  poverty caused by, 73–77
    con, 78–81
  treatment of, in welfare reform, 135
Substance Use Among Welfare Recipients: Trends and Policy Responses (Joint Center for Poverty Research), 79
suicide bombers, 158, 164–65
  see also terrorism
Supplemental Security Income, 81
Supreme Court, U.S., 95

Talbott, Strobe, 158
Tanner, Michael, 123
Taussig, Hal, 129
Taylor, John, 99
technology, 179, 186, 190, 191
teen pregnancy
  need to discourage, 58, 61
  reduction in rates of, 64
  reduction in stigma of, 62–63
Temporary Assistance for Needy Families (TANF), 79–80, 91–92, 134–36, 138–40
terrorism, 164–66
  Bush administration policy against, 175
    through loans to poorly developed countries, 177
    through trade, 176
  global poverty a cause of, 158–61
  religious/political fanaticism a cause of, 162–63
Thompson, Tommy, 135–37
Thurman, Uma, 66
transportation, 13, 81, 83, 90, 92
Tuccille, J.D., 122
Tucson, 50

Understanding Health Disparities Against Education Groups (Goldman and Lakdawalla), 43–44
unemployment, 64, 150, 181, 182, 183
United Kingdom, 42
United Nations (UN), 156–57, 165, 173, 177, 187
  Food and Agriculture Organization (FAO), 190, 191, 195, 198–99
  Human Development Index, 170, 180, 181
  Human Poverty Index, 169
United States, 136, 175, 192
  deterioration of cities in, 53–54
  genetically modified crops grown in, 196
  health care in, 29, 30
    compared to other countries, 31, 33
    need to level disparities of, 30, 34–36
  illegitimacy rates in, 60
  improved living standards in, 168
    for wealthy minority, 178
  need to increase foreign aid from, 160–61

paradox of hunger in, 19–20, 23
Urban Institute, 95–96
Us (magazine), 66
U.S. Conference of Mayors, 21, 22
U.S. News & World Report
  (magazine), 86

vagrancy, 52, 53, 54
Vásquez, Ian, 167

Wade, Robert, 178–79
Wall Street Journal (newspaper), 53,
  131, 132
War on Poverty, 114, 122, 123
Warren, Elizabeth, 57
Washington, D.C., 52, 54, 93, 98
Washington Post (newspaper), 176
water, 170, 183
Watson, Debra, 138
Wattenberg, Ben J., 187
Weicher, John C., 108
welfare participation, 74
  drug use and, 79–81
  effect of single motherhood on, 60
  freedom from poverty not
    guaranteed by, 91–92
  reduction in, 79, 86
  stereotypes about, 69–72
  unpredictability of, 85
welfare reform, 21, 48, 79, 123–24
  confusion about food stamps
    caused by, 18
  diligence a central value of, 85
  illegitimacy affected by, 64
  morality of, 87
  poor families helped by, 83–84, 86,
    134–37
    con, 138–41
  self-sufficiency a stated goal of, 89,
    135
"Welfare Reform Through a Child's
  Eyes" (*Boston Globe*), 71–72

Wennberg, John, 41–42
*What Do We Really Know About
  Whether Health Insurance Affects
  Health?* (Levy and Meltzer), 45–46
White, Vanna, 66
*Why Is Health Related to Socioeconomic
  Status? The Case of Pregnancy and
  Low Birth Weight* (Meara), 40–41
Wicks, Judy, 129
Will, George, 67
Winner, Jeanne, 148
Wolf, Martin, 169
Wolfensohn, James, 163
women, 35, 181
  as business owners, 105–107
  illiteracy and, 14
  minimum wage raise a benefit for,
    128
  poverty affects more severely than
    men, 13–14
Women, Infants, and Children
  (WIC) program, 26
Women's Center for Education and
  Career Advancement (WCECA),
  89
Woodstock Institute, 99
Wooldridge, Adrian, 174
World Bank, 169–70, 173, 177–78,
  181
World Food Summit, 190
World Health Organization
  (WHO), 157
World Socialist Web Site, 138
World Trade Organization, 178, 179

Yale Center for the Study of
  Globalization, 158
Yellen, Janet, 62–63
Youssef, Sarah, 124

Zoellick, Robert, 176